10 Classic Alpine Climbs of Japan

Tony Grant

(CLIMB JAPAN)

Copyright © 2016 Tony Grant

All Rights Reserved

ISBN-13: 978-1530110407
ISBN-10: 1530110408

Front cover photo: Final metres to the North summit of Mt Kashimayari, by Tony Grant, April 2015

Back cover photos: Mt Maehotaka N ridge, by Tony Grant, Sept 2014 / Mt Tsurugi, by Tony Grant, Sept 2014

CONTENTS

4	Disclaimer
5	Introduction
7	Geography
9	Protection on Japanese routes
11	The Kitakama ridge of Mt Yari
20	Mt Tanigawa and the infamous Ichinokura-sawa
23	The South ridge of Mt Tanigawa
28	Kamoshika
29	The North ridge of Mt Maehotaka
40	Onsen
42	The Central arête of Mt Tanigawa
47	Monkeys
49	The Main ridge of Mt Shirouma
57	Kyūya Fukada and the 'Nihon Hyakumeizan'
59	The Kitadake Buttress
67	The thunder bird
68	The O-ren-dani right fork of Mt Kaikoma
77	Japanese mountain greetings
78	The East ridge of Mt Kashimayari
85	Emergency
86	The Henkei chimney of Mt Tanigawa
92	The mountain hut system
94	The Left ridge of the Chinne on Mt Tsurugi
103	Appendix 1: Glossary of Japanese mountain words
105	Appendix 2: Route log
107	Appendix 3: Selected additional climbs
124	Further Information
125	Acknowledgements

Disclaimer

If you're a non-Japanese and you're giving serious thought to a climbing trip in this wonderful country, with all the linguistic, cultural and logistical challenges that can entail, then it can probably be said that you're a motivated individual, resourceful, imaginative and looking for a deep experience.

But let's not forget the fundamentals too. Climbing is dangerous. As Gaston Rebuffat famously remarked, "the mountain does not know you are an expert". You can train your body and mind, plan every aspect of your trip, and bad things can still happen out there.

Whilst I have put every care into assembling the information in this book, and make it a personal policy not to document in detail routes that I haven't climbed myself, once you're on the mountain you're entirely responsible for yourself. Protection on routes can change, holds break off, rocks collapse, and the Japanese mountains are subjected to huge variances of temperature, humidity, precipitation and snowfall every year. Exercise your own judgement out there, and always be prepared to turn back.

Most of all have fun and come home safely.

Introduction

The Japanese came relatively late to recreational mountain climbing. Their first alpine club, the 'Sangaku-kai', was only formed in 1905 by Kojima Usui and friends. In fact, popular culture still records that it was a foreigner, Walter Weston, who coined the term 'The Japan Alps' for the high central ranges of Honshu Island. By the time the Japanese started to make their mark in the European Alps, with the important first ascent of the Eiger's Mittellegi ridge by Yuko Maki's party in 1921, many of the classic ridges and faces of the Alps had already been climbed.

But the Japanese are a strong-willed and resourceful people, and they caught up quickly. By now most of the well-known giants of the Himalaya are home to a Japanese route, often established in winter. Big names like Uemura[1], Yamanoi[2] and Hasegawa[3] come with suitably large stories attached to them. And recent Japanese activity in the alpine has resulted in its own tales of high achievement by the *Giri Giri Boys*, as well as several *piolet d'or*[4] awards.

But what is less well-known to most people is the depth of climbing history that is written on the crags and mountains of the Japanese homeland. The average person is familiar with the graceful iconic profile of Mt Fuji, but little beyond that finds its way out.

Until this last decade, and the establishment of a healthy blogging scene, information about Japan's mountains was largely locked up in the Japanese language. For the Japanese mountaineer there are guidebooks for every branch of mountain activity, a rich and deep literature detailing the exploits of their home-grown heroes and legends on the ridges and walls of their mountains, and an exhaustive culture of online trip reports detailing ascents and conditions year round. But if a non-Japanese-speaker wanted to come to Japan and climb a classic alpine route, or a multi-pitch rock route, how were they to find the necessary information?

This book is a natural continuation of my efforts to address that situation over the last 8 years, predominantly through my own website, Climb Japan. In these pages you will find all the information you need to go out and climb ten of the finest alpine and multi-pitch classics that Honshu Island and the Japan Alps have to offer. It is by no means an exhaustive or definitive selection, but I think few would argue over the quality of the routes I've chosen.

But climbing in Japan is far more than just the mountains and the routes. You'll probably start out in one of the busiest cities of the world, a stark contrast to the wilds you're heading for. A typical trip to the mountains here will give you the chance to eat some fine rural Japanese cuisine; if you're lucky you'll see monkeys, Japanese serow, rock ptarmigans and many other species of wildlife indigenous to these islands; you'll be immersed in the environment of Japanese Shintoism and Buddhism, religions that are deeply connected with the landscape and the mountains; and at the end of it all you'll soak your tired muscles in one of the many onsen hot springs that these volcanic islands are renowned for.

I hope that this book helps you to unlock all of that, and to have an unforgettable experience, by providing the central piece of the puzzle on which all the rest will hang. We are, after all, climbers.

Notes:
  Naomi Uemura is most famous for making the first solo ascent of Denali in North America, and for his death after his bold first winter ascent of the same mountain in Feb 1984.
[2] Yasushi Yamanoi climbed a new route solo on the SW face of Cho Oyu, as well as summiting Broad Peak, Gasherbrum 2 and many other notable climbs around the world.
[3] Tsuneo Hasegawa climbed the three great north faces of the Eiger, Matterhorn and Grandes Jorasses solo and in winter.
[4] 2011: The south-east face of Mt Logan (Canada), climbed by Yasushi Okada and Katsutaka Yokoyama.
2013: The south pillar of Kyashar (Nepal), climbed by Tatsuya Aoki, Yasuhiro Hanatani and Hiroyoshi Manome.
2009: The south-west face of Kamet (India), climbed by Kazuya Hiraide and Kei Taniguchi, and the north face of Kalanka (India), climbed by Fumitaka Ichimura, Yusuke Sato and Kazuki Amano.

Geography

All of the routes in this book are located on Honshu Island, the largest and most central island of the Japanese archipelago. They are either in or not far from the Japan Alps, which run north to south down the centre of the island.

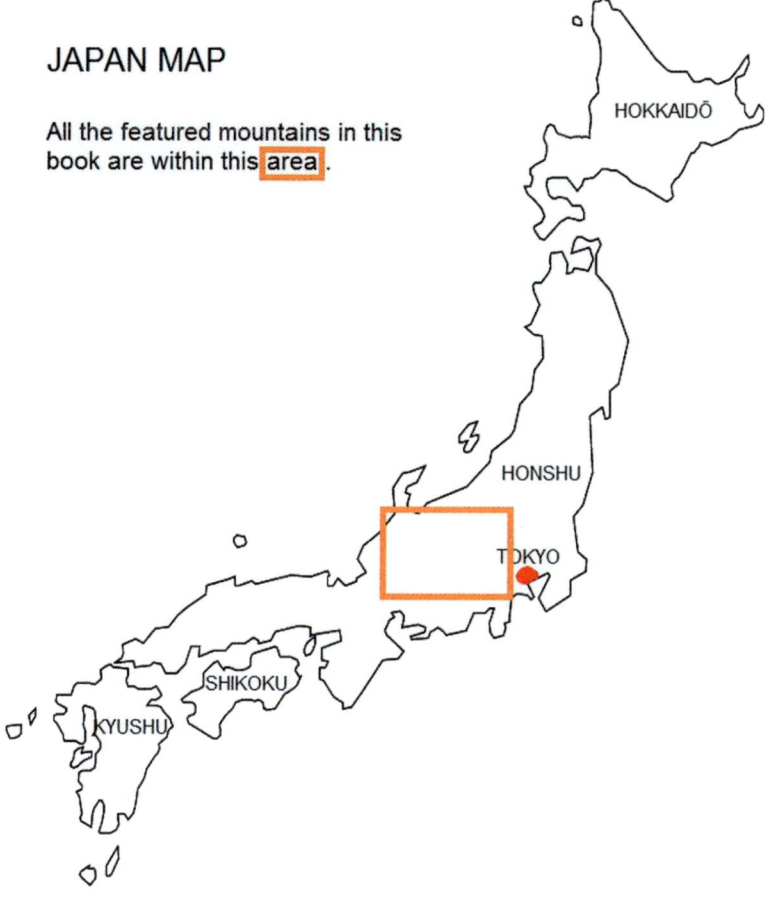

Access information in this book is provided on the assumption that most visiting climbers using this book will be starting their journey from Tokyo.

(Map data © OpenStreetMap contributors)

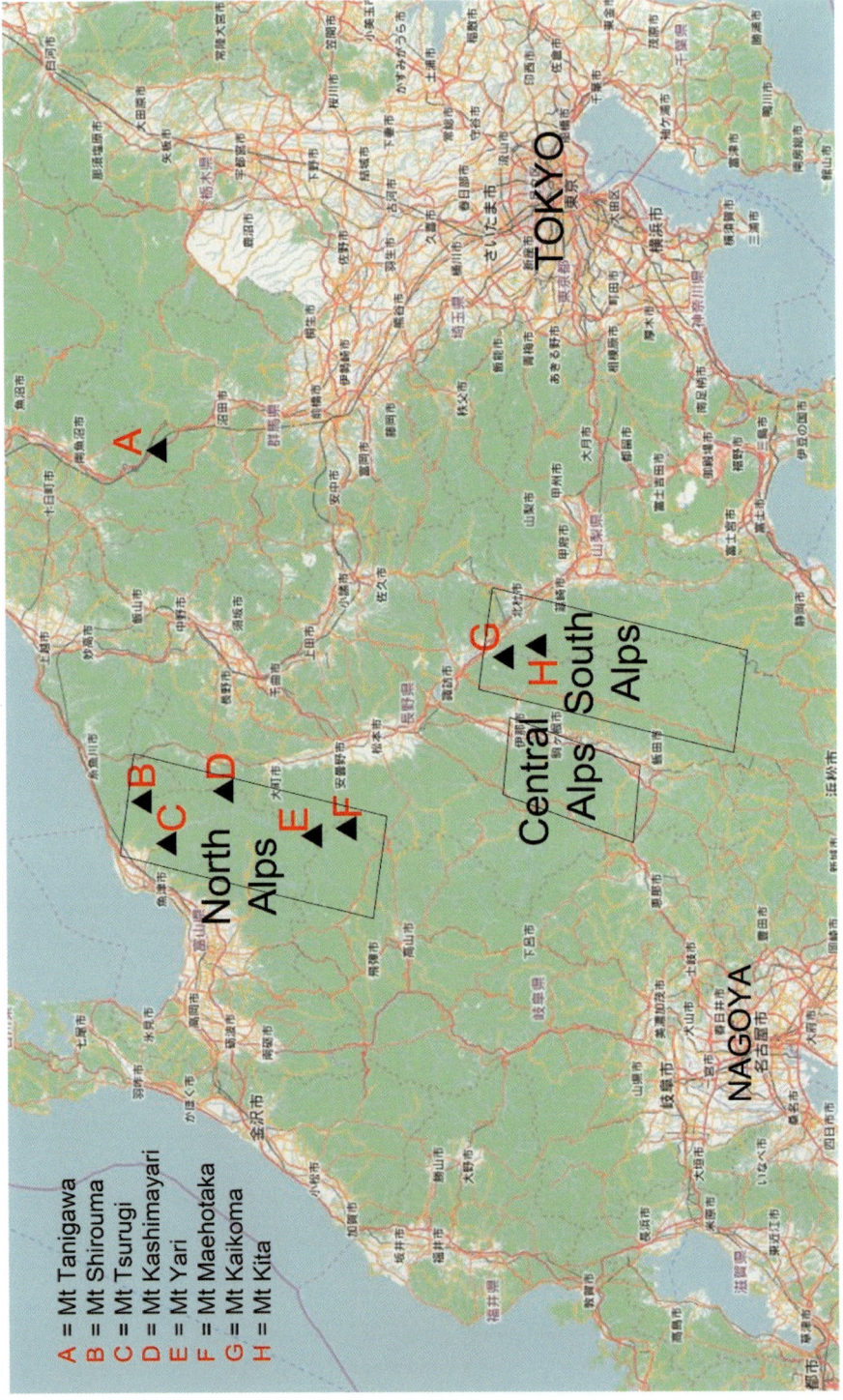

Protection on Japanese routes

Most routes in Japan have in-situ protection, usually either pitons or bolts. In most but not all cases this is due to the difficulty of finding good placements in the predominant volcanic and andesitic rock types. Depending on when the route was first climbed or the protection put in place, it will be of varying reliability.

Shiny new stainless steel bolts can be found out there, but more often than not it will be aging and rusted pitons or ring bolts. As with anywhere in the world, treat in-situ gear with healthy suspicion, and consider placing your own protection wherever possible.

An array of fixed protection:

Learn to embrace *haimatsu*, the native species of dwarf pine that can often be found on alpine ridges. A sling larks-footed around the slender but tough trunk of one of these has provided solace to many a climber on spring alpine ridges here.

THE ROUTES

1. The Kitakama ridge of Mt Yari
槍ヶ岳北鎌尾根

Route Name: Kitakama ridge (北鎌尾根)

Mountain: Yarigatake (槍ヶ岳 3180m)

Map sheet: 37 [Yama-to-kougen-chizu (山と高原地図) series]

Difficulty: Mostly rock scrambling, but lots of exposure, plenty of fixed gear if you prefer to use a rope

Mt Yari (The spear) has four major ridges extending out from its rocky summit pyramid, each following one point of the compass. These four ridges are Higashikama (東鎌), Yarihotaka (槍穂高), Nishikama (西鎌) and Kitakama (北鎌) to the east, south, west and north, respectively.

Viewed in its entirety from Kagami-daira on the ridge between Mt Kasa and the Sugoroku hut, the Kitakama ridge is breathtakingly elegant. The eye is naturally drawn from the Kitakama Col, up over the Doppyou and along to the shoulder, before shooting up the summit pyramid to the point of Yari's spear. It is quite simply one of the most beautiful sights in Japan.

During the golden years of Japanese alpinism it claimed the lives of several famous climbers, in the process attaining a reputation that, rightly or wrongly, it still holds today.

If Mt Yari is dubbed 'the Matterhorn of Japan', I would argue that this is not strictly on account of its shape or stature, but is rather due to the startling similarity of the terrain on its Kitakama ridge and summit pyramid to that of the classic ridgelines of the Matterhorn, and its perfect elegance from a distance.

The approach:
There are several ways to approach the Kitakama, but the most common are as follows:

1. From the Takase dam (高瀬ダム), several hours walk before the huts at Yumata-onsen-seiransō (湯俣温泉晴嵐荘). This is a common approach for a winter/spring ascent.

2. From Kamikōchi (上高地), up the normal hiking trail to Yarigatake, but heading up to the Minamata Col on the right 1.5hrs map time after the Yarisawa (槍沢) hut. From the Minamata Col, head straight down the slope on the other side and along for an hour or two to the Kitakama-deai.

3. From Nakafusa-onsen (中房温泉), up to the Enzansou hut on the Omote-Ginza ridgeline just below Mt Tsubakuro, along past Mt Otensho and down Bimbozawa to the Kitakama-deai.

The transportation will be slightly different for each approach, but here I'll focus on number 3, from Nakafusa-onsen.

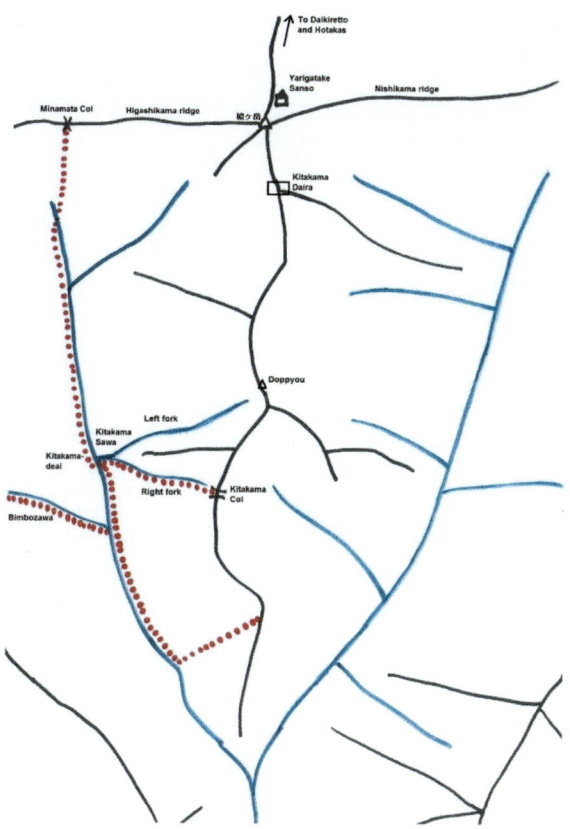

From the hut above the carpark at Nakafusa-onsen (1450m), the path rises on a well-marked trail up a series of steep zig-zags. After 3 hours map time you'll arrive at the Kassen-goya hut. Continue up for another hour of map time and you'll reach the Enzansou hut (燕山荘) at 2704m. This beautiful hut lies just a few minutes below the summit of Mt Tsubakuro (燕岳) to the north, and was built in 1921, making it one of the oldest in Japan.

The views from here are simply stunning, and if you're lucky enough, you'll get one of the finest sunsets around behind Mt Washiba (鷲羽岳) and Mt Suisho (水晶岳) across the valley!

From the Enzansou hut, head south along the Omote-Ginza ridgeline for 1h50m map time.

You'll come to a descent with a short chain/ladder section at the bottom, and shortly after this there'll be a fork in the trail below Mt Otensho (大天井岳). Take the right fork for half an hour to the Otensho hut.

The entrance to Bimbozawa (鬢乏沢) lies about half an hour beyond the Otensho hut, and is marked by an old wooden signpost.

It takes anywhere from 1.5 to 3 hours to cover the 700m descent of Bimbozawa, depending on your pace. It's not difficult, and the trail is pretty clear as long as you keep looking for it.

About 2/3 down you'll hit water, and generally the trail stays on the left side of the stream from there. At one point near the bottom there is a slab with a green fixed rope hanging down it, but it's not high and the rope is quite unnecessary.

Eventually you'll reach the exit of Bimbozawa, marked by a large piece of pink tape hanging from a branch (Note: It goes without saying though that this pink tape might not be there forever, so don't rely solely on this to know where you are.)

As you enter the main Amagami river valley, turn left and walk up for around half an hour along the boulder-covered river bed. There are reassuring cairns in places along the riverbed, but it's easy to follow.

You will shortly reach the Kitakama-deai, a broad area in the riverbed with spaces for tents among the boulders. Many people choose to camp here, and then climb the ridge to Yari the following day.

The Deai marks the entrance to the Kitakama-sawa. Walk up the boulders in this sawa, and after about 10 minutes you will come to a fork. If you realise you've been going for much more than 10 minutes and haven't found the fork, turn around and go back to try again. It really is not far up the sawa. It is vital that you take the right fork!

Take this right fork, and then head up an easy but steepening trail to gain about 700m in height. After between 1-1.5 hours you'll pull over onto the Kitakama col. There is room for one or two small tents here. Take a moment to savour being here, as this is the start of your climb.

The climb:
The first hour or so from the Kitakama Col follows a very clear hiking trail, up a mix of mud, tree routes and easy rock. It is steep in places, as you are ascending to the base of the Doppyou peak, but is easy to follow. Enjoy the views across to the crumbling yellow rock of the Iou ridgeline to the northwest, and to the perfect triangular pyramid of Mt Jōnen to the southeast.

Once you arrive at the Doppyou traverse, things get more interesting. A path will take you on a rising traverse up to the bottom right corner of the Doppyou.

From there you'll need to make a short exposed move round the corner, and then across a very narrow but well-featured ledge. There is a piton at the start of this move, in case you feel you'd like a belay across the traverse.

Midway across the traverse:

Once over the ledge, continue on to the foot of a short chimney with fixed gear. Climb this chimney, then continue along and up onto the pinnacles, following the clearest trail you can find.

The ridge continues north, and then swings round slightly to the northwest, before turning north again. I won't describe this section in too much detail, as I don't want to detract from your sense of enjoyment of the route.

In brief though, continue along the trail for a couple of hours by choosing the route that appeals most to you. In many places there are paths skirting round the pinnacles on the west (climber's right) side of the ridge, but you can stick to the ridge top the whole way, scrambling up and over all the pinnacles if you like. This is a much more enjoyable way to do it.

The climbing is always involving and interesting, but never too difficult. If you prefer the security of a rope, there are plenty of options for natural protection, and abseil points at the top of all the down climbs.

Eventually you will come to the historic Kitakama-daira, a flat area on the shoulder below the final summit pyramid. There is room here for a couple of tents. Be warned that this is no place to be caught in bad weather or a storm, and good climbers have met their end here in such circumstances.

From Kitakama-daira continue scrambling up large jumbled boulders to the start of the final climb up the left arête of the summit pyramid. The climbing on the pyramid looks complex from below, but is never difficult, and a path always presents itself up the rocks.

About 3/4 up you will come to the first of two chimneys. There is fixed gear hanging down it, and you can climb it via the easier left crack and then a traverse across into the main chimney, or tackle it straight on up the vertical right crack. It's well featured with holds, but as always on this ridge, if you prefer a rope, there is plenty of scope for gear, both fixed and natural.

A short way above the first chimney you will reach what many regard as the crux of the Kitakama, the final chimney to the summit. The exposure is tremendous, but the chimney is well-featured, and a few bridging moves will bring you to the top, from where a final short scramble will bring you out onto the summit of Yari from behind the shrine. If there are any hikers on the summit, prepare to be photographed and treated with astonishment as you pop into view!

Summary:
A classic North Alps climb, rich in the history of Japanese alpinism, and highly rewarding. The climbing is never particularly difficult, so it's not the most technically challenging of the classic alpine ridges, but the Kitakama is remote and serious and there is plenty of potential to get into trouble out there if you're not prepared.

This route is typically done in 2 or 3 days, but nowadays it is also not uncommon to complete it in a single push in under 24 hours from trailhead to trailhead. Choose your strategy according to your strengths, and then revel in the pure joy of following in the footsteps of the greats, along one of the most beautiful and aesthetic ridgelines in Japan!

JAPAN EXTRAS - 1

Mt Tanigawa and the infamous Ichinokura-sawa

The Ichinokura-sawa valley (一ノ倉沢) is one of the most striking and photographed valleys in Japan, and for very good reason. Steep ridgelines and cliffs seem to fan out geometrically from a central point in a kind of inverted horizon, lifting your eyes upwards towards the sky in a visual "bid for freedom", an escape from the claustrophobic captivity of the valley floor. It is both an inspiring and intimidating place, and people come from all over Japan to capture this sensation on film.

Ichinokura-sawa has a different face for all seasons. Located on Mt Tanigawa (谷川岳), which forms the prefectural border between Gunma and snowy Niigata, it receives huge dumps of snow every winter. Its colours are reduced to the striking black and white of rock, snow and ice.

The snow stays until early summer, and then the valley explodes in green. Autumn comes with vivid reds, browns and yellows, and the place seems almost friendly for a while. The first snows of early November complete the cycle, and the winter silence descends again.

Ichinokura-sawa is a true mountaineer's valley; it is a dead end, no hiking trails here! There is simply no way out other than the way you entered, unless you feel like climbing out. In that sense, if you can exit this valley by the summit ridgeline then you have achieved something special.

This place comes with a reputation though. In the heyday of Japanese alpinism during the 60s and 70s the sleepy station of Doai was a thriving entry point to 'Tani' for hundreds of alpinists every weekend, throwing themselves at every available line and feature. Incredible feats were accomplished, legendary routes like the *Tsuitate* pyramid.

But when so many people are treading the line in such a place, a high cost is often sadly inevitable, and the memorial cemetery at the base of the mountain near Doai testifies to the lives lost. Mt Tanigawa has a reputation as a killer mountain, with more lives lost than on any other single mountain in the world, the vast majority of those in Ichinokura-sawa.

But the topography of the place speaks for itself, and as the testing ground for generations of Japanese alpinists, I have chosen to include three classic routes from Ichinokura-sawa in this book. Climb them all, and you will understand why…

2. The South ridge of Mt Tanigawa
谷川岳南稜

Route Name: South ridge (Nanryō 南稜)

Mountain: Ichinokuradake (一ノ倉岳 1974m)

Map sheet: 16 [Yama-to-kougen-chizu (山と高原地図) series]

Length: 7 pitches + 200m simul-climbing to the summit

Time: 6-8 hours to the summit

Grade: V (IV+ A0) / Overall grade 3+ alpine climb

Getting there:
From Tokyo take the Takasaki Line for about 1.5 hours to Takasaki (高崎). Change for the Jōetsu Line for about 45 minutes to Minakami (水上), and then take a local for two stops to Doai (土合). From the underground platform at Doai station, climb a 489-step staircase from hell to reach ground level. Exit the station and join the main road, turning right and walking under a railway bridge. Follow this road for about 20 minutes up to the Visitors Centre.

Description:
This magnificent route is situated at the far end of the Ichinokura-sawa valley, which is a big draw for photographers of mountain scenery in all seasons of the year. The approach in summer takes several hours from the mouth of the valley, including one section where the trail leads high up on the left-hand side before descending again via a 50m rappel. From the bottom of the rappel a scramble takes you up to the start of the Tail ridge.

Looking up Tail ridge to the magnificent Tsuitate pyramid:

Climb Tail ridge to the top where it meets the start of the Central arête (Chuo-ryō 中央稜), then make an exposed scramble up on the left of the Central arête, a traverse across the top of the next valley on granite slab, then a short climb up to the belay ledge at the bottom of the South ridge. This small terrace marks the start of the route, and if you are planning to rappel the route after climbing then rucksacks can be left here.

Pitch 1: A short rising traverse up the wall and rightwards brings you to a chimney. Make the tricky move to enter the chimney, then climb up it and out to a belay on the left. (30m IV)

Pitch 2: Climb straight up on small but positive holds, with piton protection, for about 15m before heading up and left to a good belay stance. (25m IV)

Pitch 3: Walk / Scramble up the grassy trail with easy rocky sections to gain the belay. (40m II)

Pitch 4: Climb the short wall to the left to a spectacular belay with views down to the foot of the valley and to the walls all around. (20m III)

Pitch 5: Climb up about 10m before choosing either the left or the right of two possible routes around a promontory, then carry on up to a belay at the foot of a chimney crack. (30m III)

Pitch 6: 15m of fairly physical climbing brings you to the top of the crack. Continue to belay on a ledge below the final headwall. (25m IV)

Pitch 7: Easy climbing gains the headwall (long sling around obvious spike for protection). From here it is 10m of hard climbing up the wall, with plentiful pitons for protection. Most people climb this section A0, pulling on one of the pitons to pass through the crux move at about two-thirds height. Belay on the ledge at the top. (20m V or IV+A0)

The Eboshi rock from the top of the Nanryō:

From the top, the route can be rappelled back to the first belay ledge in 6 rappels up to 40m each on good in-situ anchors.

Continuing to the top is highly recommended if summits are important to you, but beware that the 200m of gradeless scrambling that the Japanese guidebooks describe is not entirely accurate.

In fact, from here to the summit there are still a good few hundred metres of height-gain to be made, and around 3 hours of scrambling, including several more pitches of albeit straightforward climbing on loose rock, and one final rock step before the last 100m of bush-whacking up to the top.

From the summit of Ichinokuradake, follow the hiking trail along for about 1.5/2 hours to the hut below the summit of Tomanomimi (トマノ耳), then down to Tenjindaira (天神平).

If you have missed the final cable-car from Tenjindaira, then your descent from Ichinokuradake back down to the Visitors Centre will probably take about 4-5 hours, making this a long but extremely rewarding and adventurous day in the mountains.

Summary:
An absolute local classic in one of the most beautiful mountain valleys in Japan. Seven pitches of first-class climbing on good rock, then a long but easier climb up and out to gain the highest summit of the Tanigawadake massif. Good in-situ protection, so a rack of quickdraws and a selection of nuts and long slings should suffice.

JAPAN EXTRAS - 2

Kamoshika

Sometimes, while you're walking up the approach trails in winter in Japan, you'll hear a rustling in the trees, or a sudden movement. As often as not it's a Japanese Serow, or nihon kamoshika (ニホンカモシカ).

These lovely forest-dwelling creatures are known for their speed and agility, and they are regarded as a national treasure in Japan.

If you're lucky you'll catch a glimpse of one, and if you're really lucky it will let you walk past at close proximity. Don't be afraid, they're very tame animals... Try not to startle it, they're also very shy. Just enjoy the priceless experience of meeting a large animal in its own environment.

3. The North ridge of Mt Maehotaka
前穂高岳北尾根

> **Route name**: North ridge (北尾根)
>
> **Mountain**: Mt Maehotaka (前穂高岳 3090m)
>
> **Map sheet**: 37 [Yama-to-kougen-chizu (山と高原地図) series]
>
> **Time**: 2 days (1 day approach, 1 day for the climb and descent)
>
> **Grade**: Overall grade 3 alpine route

The Hotaka range, at the southern end of the North Alps chain, is one of Japan's premier rock-climbing and scrambling destinations. Dramatic cliffs, dizzying drop-offs and knife-edge ridges abound. The range consists of five main peaks; Kitahotaka-dake (北穂高岳 3106m), Karasawa-dake (涸沢岳 3110m), Okuhotaka-dake (奥穂高岳 3190m), Nishihotaka-dake (西穂高岳 2909m) and Maehotaka-dake (前穂高岳 3090m).

The first four form a continuous ridgeline, and provide some of the most spectacular hiking experiences that Japan has to offer. To the east of this ridgeline is the famed Karasawa valley (涸沢), a steep and rocky valley that attracts photographers from all over the country during the autumn colours season. Karasawa is like a mini Annapurna Sanctuary, hemmed in on all sides by steep mountains, and it is the ridge that forms its western flank that we are interested in here.

Maehotaka-dake ('Maeho' from here on) stands off to the east of the main Hotaka ridgeline, directly in front of Kamikōchi village. From the summit a jagged ridgeline tumbles down all the way to a rocky behemoth called Byobu-no-atama (屏風の頭) at the head of Karasawa. Along the way there are 8 rocky pinnacles, ending with the summit of Byobu, and these give rise to the characteristic shape that lends its nickname among Japanese climbers - 'Godzilla's Back'.

The North Ridge is a seminal Japanese variation route, and most climbers in Japan will tread the scales of Godzilla's back at some point in their career.

Getting there:
The start point of this itinerary is Kamikōchi (上高地) in the North Alps (北アルプス). If travelling by train from Tokyo (東京) or Shinjuku (新宿), take a Super Azusa limited express train on the Chuō Line (中央線) out to Matsumoto (松本) station. From there you need to change to the Alpico Line for a 30-minute train ride to Shinshimashima (新島々). The final leg of the journey is a bus ride of about an hour from outside the train station at Shinshimashima to the alpine village of Kamikōchi, nestled at the foot of the Hotaka range in the North Alps.

Description:

There are two ways to approach the climb, so let's split this description into 3 parts, covering the two approaches separately and then the climb itself from 5-6 col to the summit, as follows:

1. Approaching up the Panorama hiking course (パノラマコース) from the Azusa river to the Byobu col (屏風のコル) at the start of the ridge itself, and climbing the first three pinnacles to the 5-6 col (the col between P5 and P6).

2. Approaching up the normal hiking trail into Karasawa, and then accessing the ridge at the 5-6 col.

3. The climb from 5-6 col to the summit.

Both approaches are good outings, although the former is more rewarding and complete in my opinion. Most people seem to favour the shorter version though.

1. The Panorama course approach
From Kamikōchi bus station, hit the hiking trail along the Azusa River. After 30-45 minutes you'll reach the Myoujin hut (明神). Keep going and after another 30-45 minutes you'll reach the large hut with campground at Tokusawa (徳沢). Keep walking for another 10-20 minutes and you'll reach a suspension bridge across the river. Cross this bridge and turn right for a few hundred metres. You'll soon reach a kind of fork, where the road turns down towards the river and a sort of ramp leads off up to the left, usually roped off. You need to take this left route to access the start of the Panorama course.

Walk up a clear trail for just over an hour and you will reach a junction. The steeper left trail leads up to a small lake below Mt Myoujin (明神岳), but you want the right hand trail. Continue up rightwards, over an intermediate ridge and a small river crossing, and you'll come to the final stretch of the trail leading up to the Byobu col. It will take up to 2 hours from the trail junction.

Be aware that there is no water on the ridge, so be sure to fill up at the last opportunity with enough to get you through the night and the next day's climb until you reach the river in Dakesawa (岳沢) on your descent.

There is space at the col for a tent, and this is a good spot to break your journey, ready to climb the ridge the next day.

To begin your ascent the next day, continue along the ridge over a small bump and you'll soon reach a junction. The Panorama course trail continues down on the right into Karasawa, but your route continues improbably directly ahead on the ridgeline.

P8: As you're still very much in tree line, the ascent of P8 involves a lot of bush-whacking and yarding up steep slopes with plenty of branches for support. Expect to get soaked if there is dew on the ground. It typically takes about an hour to reach the open grassy top.

P7: This pinnacle is more of the same, but with a little more rock scrambling thrown in. The climbing is never very difficult, but there are a few steeper sections with a little more exposure.

After the summit of P7, continue along the ridge to a small rocky pinnacle above the 7-6 col, with an in-situ rappel station. A short 15m rappel will bring you to the col.

The P7 rappel:

P6: Looking across at P6 from P7 can be a bit unnerving. It looks highly improbable, but trust me; there is a route up there. From the col you need to climb a short vertical rock-step (in-situ gear if you need it, but you probably won't). Next ascend the narrow rocky ridgeline until you reach the bulk of P6 itself, and then just follow the line of least resistance up the face.

Near the top you'll exit tree line and climb rock and jumbled boulders to the summit. A short and careful walk down will bring you to the famous 5-6 col.

2. <u>The Karasawa approach</u>
Start the same way as for the Panorama course, but continue along the Azusa river trail for another 50 minutes of map time from the suspension bridge to reach the Yokō hut (横尾). From here you need to cross the large and obvious suspension bridge and walk up the hiking trail into Karasawa.

To get into Karasawa the trail has to wind its way around the bulk of Byobu-no-atama (屏風の頭 the folding screen). The enormous rock face of Byobu-iwa (屏風岩) is home to many hard classic rock climbs.

After a couple of hours you'll reach the Karasawa hyutte (涸沢ヒュッテ) at 2300m, where you'll probably want to sleep for the night (plenty of camping available).

After an early start the next morning, head up behind the hut into Karasawa and follow a boulder trail up along the base of the north ridge. It takes about an hour from the hut to the 5-6 col, and it's a straight-forward walk up, but make sure you access the ridge from the right scree slope. You're looking for a large boulder with an arrow and "5.6 コル" in red paint.

When you reach the 5-6 col you'll join the ridge proper at the level of tree line, and from here on the climb is on rock.

3. 5-6 col to summit

P5: Keep to the ridge and scramble your way to the top, no rope needed. Enjoy the views in all directions as things start to open out.

P4: This is where things begin to get really interesting. The terrain becomes steeper, and the route is less obvious. You basically need to find your own line up to the top, following the line of least resistance.

Some might feel more secure with a rope on here, and there are anchors in place if you need them, but despite the steepness and mounting exposure, you're still only really on steep scrambling terrain in summer.

As you crest the top of P4 you'll be hit with your first up-close views of the stunning crux P3 pinnacle.

P3: The ascent of P3 is the crux section of the ridge, and this is where most climbers will be getting the rope out. There are plenty of anchors on it, and no shortage of in-situ pitons to clip into, as well as ample opportunities for placing your own trad gear.

It's entirely up to you how many pitches you want to split it into. Some topos show up to six pitches. We climbed three pitches and then simul-climbed to the top, placing runners along the way, as the climbing eased off in the upper half.

P3 pinnacle:

The crux section is near the bottom, and offers two alternatives, one being a chimney at grade IV, and the other being a slab and slanting crack at grade III. You can anchor at the same place above them, so take your pick. From the belay, climb an easier chimney crack above and then pick your line to the top of P3.

P2: In reality this is just a short scramble from the top of P3. At the summit of P2 there is a rappel station, and a short 15m rappel will bring you down to the col between P2 and the summit of Maeho.

Enjoy the position and exposure as you near the end of your climb.

P1 / Summit: A short and straight-forward scramble will bring you up to the rocky 3090m summit of Maeho. If the weather is good, take it all in… These are some of the finest views the Japanese mountains offer!

Getting down:
From the summit marker, scramble down the trail following white paint markers for about 15-20 minutes to join the main hiking trail. From here you could head right along the Tsuri-one (吊り尾根) ridge trail to Okuho if you have time, but the quickest way down is to head directly down the steep trail into Dakesawa (岳沢).

Two hours of map time will bring you to the Dakesawa hut (岳沢ヒュッテ), which sells plenty of food and drink. It's a well-known knee-crushing descent though, so take care. From the hut it's another two hours of map time down an increasingly gentle trail, at first along the sawa and then through the forest. Eventually you'll come out at the famous Kappa-bashi bridge at Kamikōchi, renowned for its views of the Hotaka range.

The bus station is a short stroll from there.

Summary:
A truly stunning and iconic ridgeline, transitioning through various alpine zones, requiring enough focus to keep things interesting but never stressful. This route is a key piece of the architecture of the Hotakas, and should be high up on the list for all Japan climbers. Bring a 50m rope, a selection of medium sized trad gear and 120cm slings, and about 6-8 extendable quickdraws.

Looking down the North ridge from the summit:

JAPAN EXTRAS - 3

Onsen

One of the first things you'll probably want to do when you get down off a big alpine route is soak your tired body in a hot bath. The good news is that Japan has got you covered.

One of the more delightful aspects of living on a volcanic archipelago is geothermal energy. All that friction from continental plates rubbing against each other creates a huge amount of heat far underground, and this results in hot water. This hot water is pumped up from underground to create Japan's mineral-rich onsen hot springs.

To find the nearest onsen, just look for the hot water symbol on Google maps or on your paper map, or on the sign outside the building if you're searching on sight.

The rules at an onsen are simple. Men and women usually bathe separately, men through the blue curtain and women through the red curtain. The onsen experience is entirely naked, no bathing costumes allowed, so leave your inhibitions at home. In Japan the bath is for relaxation, so courtesy demands that bathers wash their bodies thoroughly at the shower cubicles first. Don't worry if you don't have a towel, as most onsens will sell you one for just a few hundred yen. Traditionally most onsen resorts do not allow tattoos, but many nowadays will oblige if you cover your tattoos with a patch. If you can abide by these few simple rules, it's all good. Onsen culture is truly something special.

One more thing... Don't forget to try the outdoor bath or 'rotenburo' (露天風呂), especially in winter. There are few pleasures finer than lounging in a hot bath with snow on the ground.

4. The Central arête of Mt Tanigawa
谷川岳中央稜

Route Name: Central arête (Chuo-ryō 中央稜)

Mountain: Tanigawadake (谷川岳 1974m)

Map sheet: 16 [Yama-to-kougen-chizu (山と高原地図) series]

Length: 6 pitches (+ 150m of II/III to the summit of the Eboshi rock)

Time: 3-4 hours to the top of the last pitch

Grade: V- (IV A0) crux pitch / Overall grade 3 alpine route

This route is a 3-star (***) classic in all guidebooks, and for my money, has to be the most striking feature on Tanigawadake! No matter who looks up Ichinokura-sawa (一ノ倉沢) from below, their eyes will be drawn towards the striking arête that forms the left edge of the triangular monolith that soars up towards the Eboshi rock at the top of Tail ridge. It is an absolute must for any Tanigawa climber.

Getting there:
From Tokyo take the Takasaki Line from Ueno station for about 1.5 hours to Takasaki (高崎). Change for the Jōetsu Line for about 45 minutes to Minakami (水上), and then take a local for 2 stops to Doai (土合). From the underground platform at Doai station, climb the 489-step staircase to reach ground level. Exit the station and join the main road, turning right and walking under a railway bridge. Follow this road for about 20 minutes up to the Visitors Centre.

Description:
Walk up the road from the Visitors Centre for about an hour to the entrance to Ichinokura-sawa. Start walking up the sawa, scramble through the narrow gorge section, and after about half an hour you'll come to a seemingly impassable waterfall. A path rises up its left edge, with a fixed rope near the top. Follow this up until you come to a rappel station. Make a 25m rappel and then climb down to the sawa with the fixed ropes.

From here you can gain access to the start of Tail ridge. Scramble up to the top, with occasional fixed ropes. The bottom belay anchor of the Chuo-ryō is literally at the top of Tail ridge.

Pitch 1: Climb up and leftwards following the pitons. A short crux section at about 30m brings you to the belay anchor. (40m IV)

Pitch 2: Make a short, exposed but easy, traverse around to the left side of the arête, and then follow a sort of wide chimney to a belay. (25m III)

Pitch 3: Make a short and exposed traverse back onto the arête, then climb a groove. Deciding exactly where this pitch ends can be confusing, but there is a belay station in-situ. The crux is a thin section of IV just below the anchor, which can be aided if necessary. (25m IV)

Pitch 4: Climb up and rightwards until you gain access to a chimney. Climb up with in-situ piton protection. The chimney narrows and overhangs near the top, but an undercling allows a high move to be made out of the chimney on the left, from where easier climbing leads to the anchor, a spacious ledge with an incredible view. If you are unable to free climb it, the top moves can be done A0 with in-situ pitons. (25m V- / IV A0)

Pitch 5: An easier pitch follows up and leftwards to a comfortable belay in a kind of wide chimney. (25m III)

Pitch 6: Climb up and out of the chimney to a pinnacle with a rappel anchor on it. Continue up past the pinnacle. At this point the climbing becomes very exposed. The holds are all there, and it is not excessively difficult, but the exposure adds to the sense of difficulty. Don't be put off by the length of the pitch; there is a good anchor up there with ring bolts and pitons. (40m III+)

You have now reached the top of the difficulties, and are faced with three options:

1. Continue up 150m or so of rock at II/III and steep grass and bushes to the top of the Eboshi rock, make a rappel into a groove above the top anchor of the South Ridge (南稜), and then continue up to the summit of Ichinokuradake (一ノ倉岳). This will add considerably to the length of the day.

2. Do as above, but rappel down the South ridge on fixed anchors.

3. Call it good at the top of the 6th pitch and rappel the Chuo-ryō. This requires multiple 50m rappels, and care must be taken to ensure the ropes do not get stuck in a crack near the top of the crux chimney pitch, but this is by far the most popular option.

If you choose to rappel, then descent is simply to reverse Tail ridge and the valley below back to the car park at the start of Ichinokura-sawa.

You can now buy yourselves a cold beer in celebration of climbing one of the most classic lines in the area.

Summary:
An outright 3-star classic and a must-do on the wish list of any Tanigawa climber. Good quality rock on the whole, superb positions and exposure, and good rappel anchors. Take a small selection of nuts in addition to quickdraws, but don't be surprised if you don't use any of them. Climb it, now...

JAPAN EXTRAS - 4

Monkeys

One of the most delightful things that can happen in the Japanese high country is to come across a troop of Japanese Macaques. Known to the Japanese as "saru" (猿), these highly intelligent and mischievous monkeys have the distinction of being the most northerly non-human primates in the world, and are the only monkeys anywhere that can live in snow country.

Seemingly nothing excites people more than a sighting of these macaques, and any appearance is usually accompanied by the clicking of countless cameras. They can be seen almost anywhere, and in recent years have been making serious encroachments on village allotments in Yamanashi and Nagano prefectures, to the consternation of local farmers.

The real prize is seeing them bathing in an outdoor onsen in winter, and the best place for this is Jigokudani in the Shiga highlands.

For myself, I'll never forget an early morning in Machiga-sawa on Mt Tanigawa, when my partner and I were scrambling up the riverbed boulders towards an attempt on the East ridge and all of a sudden a troop of well over a hundred monkeys emerged from the trees and crossed the river all around us. The atmosphere was electric, and we froze to the spot, utterly outnumbered and scared stiff of doing anything to antagonise them. But they never threatened us at all, and that 10 minutes standing there as dozens of families, mothers, babies and alpha males passed by all around us, will never leave me.

5. The Main ridge of Mt Shirouma
白馬岳主稜

> **Route name**: Main ridge (Shu-ryō 主稜)
>
> **Mountain**: Shiroumadake (白馬岳 2932m)
>
> **Map sheet**: 34 [Yama-to-kougen-chizu (山と高原地図) series]
>
> **Time**: 2 days (1 day approach, 1 day for the climb and descent)
>
> **Grade**: Overall grade 2+ alpine route

The Shu-ryō is a winter/spring alpine climb, and the optimal time of year for it is April. Before then you will find a lot of snow, and access will be more difficult. After the Golden Week holidays of late April / early May, the chances of finding the ridge in perfect condition will go down as temperatures rise and the snow cover begins to break up. Consider all this in your planning.

Getting there:

If travelling by train from Tokyo (東京) or Shinjuku (新宿), take a Chuō Line (中央線) train out to Hakuba (白馬) station on the edge of the North Alps (北アルプス). The quickest way is to take the Super Azusa all the way, but depending on the time of day you might have to take an Azusa to Matsumoto (松本) and then change for a local train on the JR Ooito line to Hakuba.

Next take a bus from outside Hakuba station to Sarukura (猿倉). Note that the bus service only starts running in late April, in time for the opening of the hut at Sarukura and the start of Golden Week.

If travelling by car, there are parking spaces outside the hut at Sarukura or in a larger car park just before the hut. Note though that the road to Sarukura is usually closed by a locked barrier at Futamata (二股) until the day before the Golden Week holidays start, which would add an extra hour's walk to day one of this itinerary.

Description:
DAY ONE

After spending the whole morning getting to Sarukura, you'll be pleased to hear that basecamp for the Shu-ryō is reached in a gentle hour's walk. In summer there is an obvious trail to follow, but in winter/spring it's buried under the snow. If you're standing in the car park in front of the hut at Sarukura, the path goes round the side of the hut on the left.

About 20 metres beyond the hut, head up the slope for 5-10 minutes until you hit a forest road, or rindou. Follow this road to your right and it will take you up the valley into the mountains, contouring above the river. You will pass several concrete dams, and eventually your path will converge with the river as the terrain widens out into a large snow bowl as you approach the foot of the Shu-ryō.

The Shiroumajiri (白馬尻) hut is located here, but you wouldn't know it, as in spring it is still buried under tons of snow. Be aware that there is a high risk of avalanches in this area and particularly from the Daisekkei (大雪渓) above, so choose your camp spot wisely. There is a rise in the centre of the valley, about 100m from the start of the Shu-ryō's approach slopes, and this is a good area to camp, away from the valley sides.

Setting up camp at the foot of the Shu-ryō:

DAY TWO

The ridge itself is a series of rising peaks and bumps, numbered in sequence from P8 at the top of the approach slopes all the way up to P1, the summit itself. Connecting these peaks is a thrilling knife-edge snow ridge, with a total height-gain from basecamp to summit of approximately 1400m.

The line of the Shu-ryo:

Depending on the line you choose, it should take up to a couple of hours to climb the initial slopes and gain the ridge itself at P8. Once on the ridge, the way to go is obvious. Take care to stay well away from the cornices on climber's right between P8 and P7.

Up to about P5 you can find tree anchors if you need them, but from there onwards you are on your own as things open out. Around this point, as the character of the route morphs into a pure snow climb, the exposure begins to mount on all sides and the ridge takes on the atmosphere of a much bigger climb.

The knife-edges become sharper, the drops on both sides larger and as you get into the East face proper and approach P3 and P2, the ridge begins to rear up more steeply.

In good years it's quite common that parties will not need to get the rope out until P3 or P2, but conditions can vary from year to year and depending on how early or late in the season you are there, so be prepared to pitch these latter sections on your own snow belays if necessary.

Eventually you will arrive at the small flat area on top of P2, the final resting spot before the crux section of the route; the headwall for which the Shu-ryō is deservedly famous.

This final slope is approximately 60m high, and steepens up to an angle of about 60 degrees in its upper half. It is always overhung by an enormous cornice. Some parties choose to climb the exit slope in one full rope length, but there are rock anchors available around halfway up the slope if you prefer to split it into two pitches. Placing a snow stake before the final cornice will also add a measure of security in the event of a slip.

One of the many attractions of the Shu-ryō is that you top out right on the summit itself, near the concrete summit marker. The feeling of pulling over that cornice and topping out onto the relatively flat summit area is priceless.

On a clear day you will be able to see all the way across to Tsurugidake (剱岳) and as far out as Yarigatake (槍ヶ岳) to the south. Congratulate yourselves on a great climb before you begin the walk down.

Getting down:
There are a few ways you could get down from the summit, but all except one take substantially longer and more effort and will not bring you back to your tent. The quickest and easiest way down to your tent is to go down the Daisekkei (Great Snow Valley 大雪渓), but this is very avalanche-prone in spring and if you choose to take this route down, treat it with full respect and get it done as quickly and as safely as you possibly can.

From the summit, head south to the enormous Hakuba-sansou (白馬山荘), about 10-15 minutes below. Continue down the same way until you reach the next big hut at the top of the Daisekkei. The route swings to the east now on climber's left and drops down into the Daisekkei. If you're fast you can be through all this and back to your tent in about an hour from the summit, but it may take longer. Keep your eyes and ears open and alert for avalanches.

From Shiroumajiri and your tent, all that remains is to reverse the hour's walk back down to Sarukura.

Summary:
Easily one of the most aesthetic itineraries in Japan, the Shirouma Shu-ryō is the classic snow line. It has both ambience and exposure, and for a route of only moderate difficulty it demands fitness, a head for heights and the ability to protect yourselves on steep snow. This is without a doubt one of the classic climbs of the Japan Alps!

Summit satisfaction:

JAPAN EXTRAS - 5

Kyūya Fukada and the 'Nihon Hyakumeizan'

In 1964 the Japanese alpinist Kyūya Fukada published a book, "Nihon Hyakumeizan" (日本百名山), in which he proposed a list of the one hundred finest mountains in Japan. His list was an entirely subjective one, based on three criteria; grace, history and individuality. In general the mountains had to weigh in at over 1500m in altitude, although there are notable exceptions to this rule within the list.

Over time this has become the accepted tick list for Japanese hikers, much like the Munroes of Scotland, and the Wainwrights of the English Lake District. There are now countless guidebooks detailing the easiest way to tackle each mountain, and the peaks themselves are all marked on the Yama-to-kougen-chizu (山と高原地図) hiking map series as '百名山'.

The North Alps and the Chūbu region are the most heavily represented on the list, being Fukada's home region. But the geographical spread of the mountains encompasses the full length of Japan from Mt Miyanoura on Yakushima Island (屋久島) in the south, all the way up to Mt Rishiri at the north-western tip of Hokkaido Island (北海道). Thousands of Japanese hikers make it their life's hobby to try and climb all one hundred mountains, and nowadays there is an extensive network of hiking trails and mountain huts and lodges to facilitate this. The Japan Tourism Agency would be very hard pushed to dream up a better initiative to promote the far corners of the country!

In 2015 the list got an international boost in the form of an English translation of Fukada's book, painstakingly put together by Martin Hood under the title "One Hundred Mountains of Japan". If you are interested in completing the hyakumeizan yourself, I recommend buying a copy of his translation for historical interest, as well as subscribing to his excellent blog "One Hundred Mountains".

Fukada's final list has proved controversial over the years, with many feeling that some notable mountains were missed off in favour of lesser peaks, but in my opinion one thing is indisputable; the hyakumeizan will provide you with a first-rate framework for exploring this beautiful country and a delightful project that could keep you busy for years.

6. The Kitadake Buttress
北岳バットレス

Route name: No.4 ridge 'The Buttress' (第四尾根 バットレス)

Mountain: Mt Kitadake (北岳 3192m)

Map sheet: 41 [Yama-to-kougen-chizu (山と高原地図) series]

Time: 2 days (1 day approach, 1 day for the climb and descent)

Grade: VI (III A1) / Overall grade 3 alpine route

At 3192m, Mt Kitadake (北岳) has the distinction of being Japan's second highest mountain after Mt Fuji (富士山). Its east face is home to a series of gullies and a striking 600m rock face, known to all Japanese climbers simply as 'The Buttress' (バットレス). There are several routes up it, but here we'll concern ourselves with the central piece to the Buttress, the uber-classic No.4 ridge.

First climbed in 1934, the No.4 ridge is a sharp arête that seems to hang suspended up the centre of the face drawing the eye to the summit.

The purple rock is a type of chert, downward-sloping and largely friction-less, distinct from the more friendly rock types found in other areas of Japan's alpine ranges. It's not a good place to be in rain or poor weather, so make sure you have a stable forecast.

In 2011 there was a major rock fall in the upper section, and the final pitch of No.4 ridge fell down. Consequently the finish to the route is now substantially harder and more satisfying. The area is far from 100% stable though, and more large rock falls can probably be expected in the future. In short, if you haven't climbed this route yet, hurry up before it gets consigned to the history books!

Getting there:
If travelling by train from Tokyo (東京) or Shinjuku (新宿), take a Chuō Line (中央線) train out to Kōfu (甲府) station. Ideally you want to be on the first Super Azusa limited express train in the morning.

Next you need to take a bus from the bus stands outside Kōfu station via the Yashajin Pass (夜叉神峠) to Hirogawara (広河原). The bus ride takes approximately two hours. You will begin your approach from Hirogawara.

Description:
From the bus stop at Hirogawara walk up the road for a couple of minutes, then cross the suspension bridge over the river. Walk up the trail for about 15-20 minutes and you'll come to a junction, and the trail you take depends on where you're planning to sleep.

If you're going to spend the night in the Shiraneoike hut (白根御池小屋) then take the right fork, and you'll arrive at the hut in a couple of hours. If you're planning to bivvy below the route, take the left fork, and follow the hiking trail up the river.

After a couple of hours the sawa opens out and you'll arrive at a junction called Futamata (二俣). From here there is a steep trail heading up to the right to the Kitadake summit ridge, and another trail contouring in from the Shiraneoike hut. You need to keep going up the sawa, sticking to the trail on the right edge.

As you climb the sawa you will start to see the east face of Kitadake opening up on your right, with its various ridges and gullies falling down to where you are. The final approach to the Buttress ascends D-gully (d ガリー), so keep your eyes open for a decent bivvy spot anywhere between the end of the water in the sawa and the entrance to the gully. Be sure to fill up all your water capacity though, as there is no water on the route itself.

D-gully access:
After an early start, hike up the trail until you reach the entrances to C and D gullies on your right. D gully provides the easiest and most direct way up to the foot of the Buttress.

Once you reach the rock, you need to climb 3 pitches up D-gully to reach a traverse ledge that will bring you to the start of the No.4 ridge itself.

Pitch 1: Climb an awkward rock step (in-situ piton to A0 the move if necessary) to gain entry to the gully, then climb about 30m with pitons at spaced-out intervals, to an in-situ anchor.

Pitch 2: Move up and diagonally right from the belay, then either break the pitch at an in-situ anchor or continue on and belay on your own gear.

Pitch 3: Climb the wet and slimy constriction above until D-gully opens out. Continue up and slightly right to the start of the traverse ledge.

Pitch 4: Traverse rightwards across the narrow scree-covered ledge, with occasional in-situ pitons. Continue around the rib and up to belay on the comfortable ledge at the start of the first pitch of No.4 ridge.

Looking back across the traverse:

Now you're in position and ready to start ascending the route proper.

No.4 ridge:
The first five or six pitches are obvious enough, and there are plenty of anchors along the way. Initially the route weaves its way up through trees on decent rock, either on the arête itself or the right side of the arête, at grade III-IV.

As you climb higher the route exits tree line, and the air and exposure kicks in. It's a fantastic place to be!

Enjoying the exposure:

Eventually you'll arrive at the belay beneath what used to be the crux pitch of the route. Climb the face for a few metres to gain the thin rightward slanting grade V crack line.

Nowadays the rock here is quite polished, and the holds are thin, but there are in-situ pitons in the crack, allowing you to aid through if necessary. Once you latch the jug hold at the top, you just need to swing out right and climb up onto the arête, and it's done.

The rest of the pitch is airy and steep, but well-featured, right on the crest of the arête. Protection is very spaced out, but there are a couple of rock spikes that will take slings. Belay at the rappel anchor on top of the famous Matchbox rock (マッチ箱).

From the top of the Matchbox, a 20m rappel will bring you down to an anchor on the upper slabs of D-gully.

From this anchor you can gain the belay at the site of the rock fall in a long pitch of almost a full 50m rope length. Climb the steep chimney crack on your right along the bottom edge of the Matchbox (grade IV), and then continue up the arête on delightful thin moves at grade III to the belay.

As previously mentioned, the final pitch of the route used to continue up the ridge on straight-forward grade III terrain, but in 2011 the entire triangular rock that housed this pitch collapsed, leaving a blank vertical face barring the way. Fortunately there was an alternative way through this upper cliff, in the form of the last pitch of D-gully out on the slabs to your left.

Accessing this last pitch involves an airy horizontal traverse across a knife-edge blade of rock to gain the D-gully slabs, and then you continue on for another 10m to reach an in-situ bolt belay on the slab. It looks outrageous, and is incredibly exposed, but there's nothing on it harder than easy grade III.

From there, the route now has one final sting in its tail; the exit pitch of D-gully, an overhanging off-width crack. Ascend the slabs to gain entry to the crack, then climb up in a very awkward position past a couple of loose bendy pitons. When the crack runs out, make a very strenuous move out to your left, with terrible feet, to gain better holds to the top. If you can climb it free, this pitch goes at grade VI, but if you can't manage that, it can be aided at III A1. Be careful with those first two pitons though, as you really wouldn't want to fall on them.

Now you just need to scramble up a final 20m of grade II rock to the end of the climbing. From here to the top, follow a trail up through the bushes for about 15 minutes and you will gain the summit ridgeline and the hiking trail, just a few metres down from the top of the mountain.

The views from the top of Kitadake are spectacular in all directions.

Getting down:
From the top you have the choice of two hiking trails to descend, one heading north and down to the Kitadake Katanogoya hut (北岳肩ノ小屋), and the other heading south to the junction with the trail across to Mt Ainodake (間ノ岳), Japan's 4th highest peak. From the junction, the trail swings east for about half an hour to another junction at the start of the Happonba ridgeline, with great views across the Buttress.

Take the descent trail heading north down chains and ladders to regain the sawa and your bivouac gear, then continue down the trail you came up on the day before to return to Hirogawara.

Summary:
A spectacular route, with superb climbing up a striking natural line, finishing on the second highest summit in Japan. This route might be the most famous alpine rock climb in all of Japan, and deservedly so. Bring a trad rack and about 12 quickdraws, and don't forget your A-game for that final pitch out of D-gully!

JAPAN EXTRAS - 6

The thunder bird

If you are out and about in the North Alps of Japan you'll have a very good chance of spotting a rock ptarmigan. With a delightful croaking call that can sound more like a frog than a bird, these protected birds are remarkably tame. They tend to live quite high up on the ridgelines, often in extremely harsh conditions.

In summer their plumage is a mottled brown and grey, but as the winter snows set in these summer feathers are replaced with a striking white. They are truly beautiful, and one of Nagano's treasures.

7. The O-ren-dani right fork of Mt Kaikoma
甲斐駒ケ岳黄蓮谷右俣

Route Name: O-ren-dani right fork (黄蓮谷右俣)

Mountain: Kaikomagatake (甲斐駒ケ岳 2967m)

Map sheet: 41 [Yama-to-kougen-chizu (山と高原地図) series]

Time: 2-3 days

Grade: Overall grade 3+ alpine route

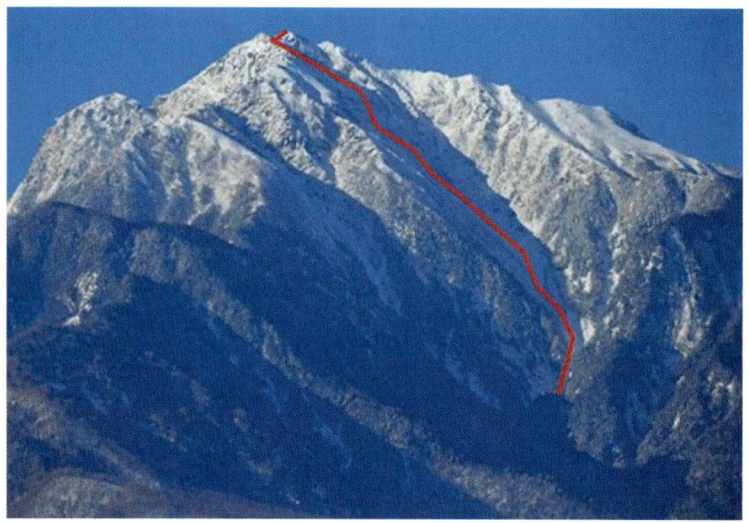

As you pass by Mt Kaikoma on a Chuo Line train the eye is forcibly drawn into the depression that cleaves its north-eastern face from bottom to top, part gully and part canyon. Beginning almost at the foot of the mountain and ending right at the summit, the O-ren-dani is immense, and instantly recognisable.

In summer a stream forms in its upper slabs, becoming a torrent as it tumbles down the mountain, and when winter arrives it freezes to form one of the most beautiful ice climbs in Japan.

Conditions are notoriously hard to predict. Get there too early in December and the ice might not be formed; get there too late and it might be buried under metres of snow, and avalanche prone. But if you can hit it just right, you can expect to be climbing on near-continuous water ice for about 1200m!

Access is complex, requiring the climber to ascend two-thirds of the Kuroto ridge, and then lose about 800m of that hard-won altitude to get in to the bottom of the route. It is not a place to have anything go wrong, so you should be well-trained and prepared.

But make no mistake… This route is a hands-down classic, and one of the most sought-after winter alpine climbs Japan has to offer.

Getting there:
If travelling by car from Tokyo (東京), take the Chuō Expressway to Sutama (須玉) and then exit onto route 141. A combination of local roads will bring you within about half an hour to the Hakushukankōjiro camping ground (白洲観光尾白キャンプ場). The car park here is the end of the road and the access point for the Kuroto ridge of Mt Kaikoma and all climbing routes on the east side of the mountain.

Description:

THE APPROACH
From the car park, walk past the barrier and continue along the rough road for about 5-10 minutes until you reach the Chiku-Komagatake shrine (竹宇駒ケ岳神社), an ancient holy site for shugendō religious practice. From the shrine, cross the suspension bridge over the river and follow the path upwards through the initial zig zags.

After about 30mins the path will veer to the left and contour up and round onto the crest of the ridge. Keep going, and after about 2 hours of map time you will reach a junction where your trail is joined by another approach trail that came up from Yokote-Komagatake shrine. You are now on the Kuroto ridge proper. Keep following the path up through the forest, with red paint markers on the trees to show you the right way.

After about 1.5 hours the ridge will begin to narrow until you reach an airy knife-edge section with chains. Cross this with care, and after another 15-20 minutes you will reach a small shrine at 2049m. From here on you will begin to encounter ladders fixed on the steep sections.

Looking back across the knife-edge section:

Keep going for another hour or so and the trail will descend for about 100m to a col. This is the 5th station on the ridge. In the past there was an emergency hut here, the Gogome-goya (五合目小屋), but this hut no longer exists.

The descent trail into the O-ren-dani starts from the 5th station. You will be passing this spot again on your way down from the summit, so you could consider camping here and picking up your tent on your way back down after your climb.

If you are not planning to camp, then you will need to continue up the ridge for another hour or so to the Shichijōdaiichi-goya hut (七丈第一小屋). The trail to the hut goes up and down very steeply, with a lot of ladders and chains to negotiate, some of them quite exposed indeed. Eventually you will round a corner at about 2400m and arrive at the hut. A night here currently costs about ¥4600 including unlimited water supplies.

THE CLIMB

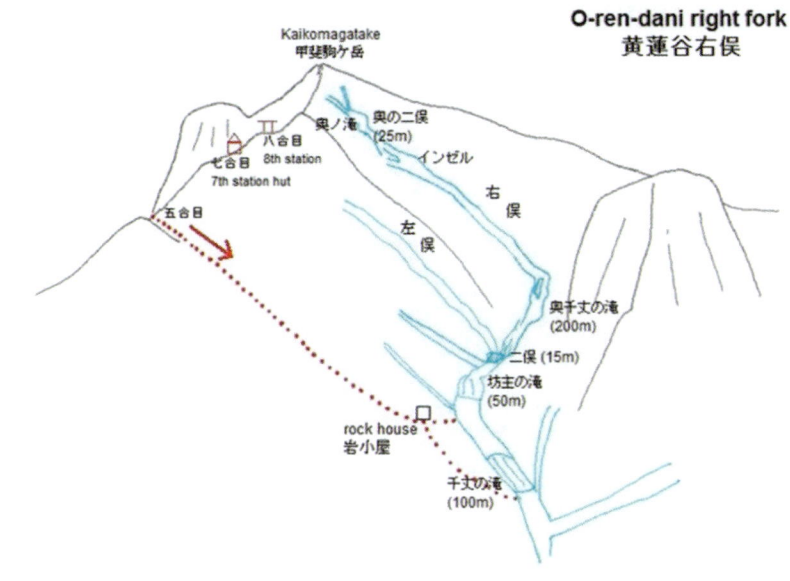

Set your alarm bright and early, because it's going to be a big day! The first hour of the day involves retracing your steps back down the chains and ladders to the 5th station. From there you are ready to drop down into the O-ren-dani.

When you arrive at the 5th station, turn left and follow the trail into the trees. At first you'll be contouring slightly to your right, and you'll soon come to a landslide gully. Cross the landslide carefully, and continue downwards until you find yourself on a forested ridge. You now need to descend this ridge, keeping towards its left side. Route-finding is not obvious in the dark, and there are no trail markers, so keep your eyes open and look for signs of passage from other climbers. There are a series of short cliffs down this ridge, which you'll need to bypass. Eventually after about 1.5 hours and numerous false turns, you should come to a large rock formation near the bottom of the sawa (岩小屋). A few metres below this you will reach the river. There is a waterfall here, but it is unlikely to be frozen, so bypass it on the left via a short scramble with a fixed rope in place.

A short way beyond, you will arrive at the first icefall of the O-ren-dani, the 50m Bōzu-no-taki (坊主の滝). This could be climbed in a single pitch with a 60m rope, but that would put you out of hearing range with your belayer, so most people climb it in two pitches.

Continue up the sawa and you will reach the 15m Futamata (二俣) icefall.

Looking down the Futamata icefall:

After this, continue up the sawa at a gentle gradient for a little while. Up ahead you will see the turn off for the O-ren-dani's left fork (左俣). Don't go up there today, but head to your right and climb a short fall. Continue up an ice ramp until you reach another steeper fall.

This is the start of the famous 200m Oku-Senjō-no-taki (奥千丈の滝). This wonderful section just seems to continue on and on with perfect water ice on all sides of you. It is breathtakingly beautiful.

Ascending the wonderful Oku-Senjō-no-taki in perfect conditions:

At the top of this section the O-ren-dani veers to climber's left in the direction of Kaikoma's summit, still about 900m above you. In good conditions you will be on water ice almost all the way, with increasingly open vistas behind you stretching across the valley to the Yatsugatake massif.

After several hours you will reach the final obstacles barring the way to the summit, the Oku-no-Futamata-no-taki (奥の二俣の滝) and the Oku-no-taki (奥ノ滝) icefalls.

The final obstacle:

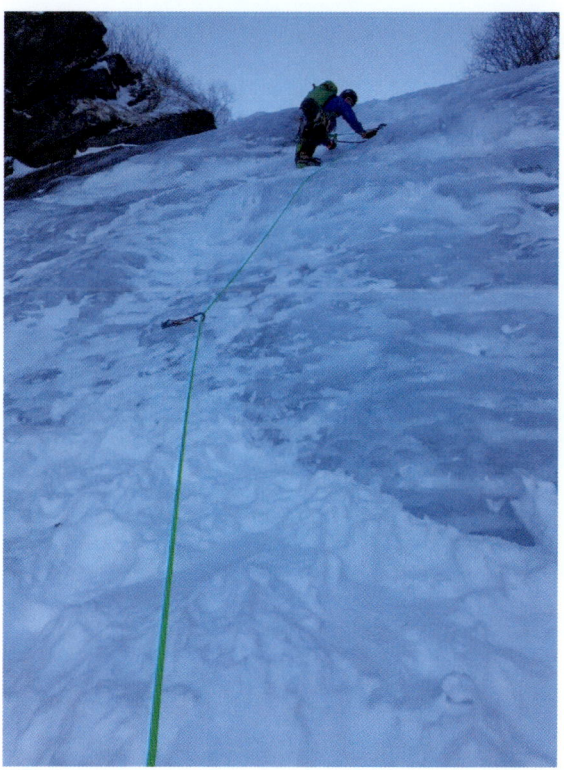

Once you've surmounted these, the O-ren-dani begins to open up a bit and you'll find yourself front-pointing up steep snow slopes for several hundred metres. Eventually you will exit onto the final 50m of the Kuroto ridge just below the summit.

A short walk will bring you to the top, with some of the finest views in Japan, taking in Kitadake and the nearby Houou-sanzan, all three of Japan's alpine ranges, and the Yatsugatake massif across the valley!

From the summit you just need to descend the 2200m of elevation down the Kuroto ridge back to the temple and the car park.

Summary:
Simply mind-blowing! Wild, remote, long and consistently exposed, the beautiful O-ren-dani is the prize of the South Alps. If you are lucky to find good conditions, you are guaranteed to have the experience of a lifetime here!

JAPAN EXTRAS 7

Japanese mountain greetings

As their reputation goes, the Japanese are a very friendly nation, and nowhere is this more apparent than in the mountains. In contrast to the way Tokyo can sometimes feel, where people are stressed and working hard, it's remarkably easy to strike up conversation with Japanese people in mountain huts and on trails. Mountains seem to have that effect on people all over the world.

To break the ice and smooth the path for you, here are a few useful phrases that you're bound to hear at some point:

Hello	*Konnichi-wa*
Good morning	*Ohayou-gozaimasu*
Isn't the weather great?	*Ii tenki desu-ne?*
Beautiful, isn't it?	*Kirei desu-ne?*
Please take care.	*O-kiyotsukette kudasai*
Where are you from?	*Dochira kara desu-ka?*
Is it okay to take a photograph?	*Shashin o-totte-mo ii desu-ka?*
Go ahead.	*Dōzō*
After you.	*O-saki ni dōzō*

8. The East ridge of Mt Kashimayari
鹿島槍ヶ岳東尾根

> **Route name**: East ridge (Higashi-one 東尾根)
>
> **Mountain**: Kashimayari-ga-take (鹿島槍ヶ岳 2889m)
>
> **Map sheet**: 35 [Yama-to-kougen-chizu (山と高原地図) series]
>
> **Time**: 1-2 days
>
> **Grade**: Overall grade 3 alpine route

Mt Kashimayari is one of the finest of Japan's North Alps giants, and one of its most distinctive.

It is situated on the long ridgeline that runs north to south from Mt Shirouma in the Hakuba area down to Ōgisawa, entry point for the famous Alpen Route through the Kurobe Dam to Mt Tateyama. Its immediate neighbour to the north is Mt Goryu, and the kirettō ridgeline that connects them contains some of the most dramatic and exposed hiking in the area.

Mt Kashimayari has twin summits connected by a bow-shaped col. The South summit (南山頂 2889m) is the higher of the two, and the 'hyakumeizan' highpoint, while the North summit (北山頂 2842m), with its East ridge, Tengu ridge (天狗尾根) and precipitous North face, is home to some of the most dramatic alpine climbing routes in the area.

In snow conditions, from late winter (March) through to around Golden Week (end of April), the East ridge (東尾根) provides one of Japan's most aesthetic and satisfying alpine climbs. Not for the faint-hearted, this is a serious and committing ridge with near-constant exposure along its entire length. The ridge shelves steeply off to the left, and unstable cornices along the crest ensure that aspirants spend their whole ascent on these inclines with the void below never really leaving your field of vision. It's an exhilarating feeling, and really does warrant this route's classic status.

Getting there:
If travelling on public transport, take a train to Shinano-Ōmachi (信濃大町) station, and then take an Ōmachi city bus bound for Gen-yū (源汲方面) and get off the bus at Kashima (鹿島) bus stop, not long after the Jiigatake ski resort (爺ガ岳スキー場). From there it is about an hour's walk to the car park at Ōtanbara (大谷原). If you don't have time to wait for one of the infrequent buses, you could also consider spending approximately ¥5500 on a taxi.

If you have a car, you need to drive to the trailhead at the end of the road at Ōtanbara. There is a toilet block and a car park with space for 10-15 cars.

Description:
Due to the amount of snow on the mountain in late winter, this route is typically climbed over two days, with a night spent in the tent on one of the pinnacles in the lower half of the route. If you're a fast party, and you find good snow conditions as we did, it can be done comfortably in a day up and down.

From the car park at Ōtanbara, cross the bridge and walk along the rindou for about 20 minutes. You'll go past a small hydro plant on the riverside, and the road will switch back at one point. You'll soon notice the ridge up on your right, and you'll come to an entry point where it's possible to ascend up to the ridgeline.

Head up the steep slope until you gain the ridge, then head left up the crest of the ridge in the trees. This continues for a couple of hours until you leave tree line, and eventually you'll arrive on top of the Ichi-no-sawa-no-atama (一の沢の頭) pinnacle at 2004m. There is space for a couple of tents up here if needed.

From here onwards you are into the climbing on the East ridge proper. Continue along a very sharp ridge, treading carefully on top of the cornices in some places where no alternative exists.

After some time you'll arrive at the Ni-no-sawa-no-atama (二の沢の頭) pinnacle, where there is again room for a couple of tents. Up to now the gradients have been relatively gentle, but from here on things are going to get much steeper.

Descend down the far side of the pinnacle and up over the next, then ascend a steep snow slope until you arrive at the foot of the first rock step. The drop-offs to climber's left are really quite substantial now, so take care as you climb.

The steeply shelving upper ridge:

The first rock step is pretty straight-forward. There is a piton anchor at the foot of it, and a 50m rope will suffice. First climb up well-featured rock, with in-situ piton protection, then get onto the snow and climb mixed ground to an anchor near the top.

You can unrope again here, but be aware that there is still a bit of easy mixed terrain remaining, and you'll exit this onto a steep snow slope with no real resting points until you gain the crest at the top.

Continue along the crest here, over a sharp snow pinnacle and down the other side. Scramble up a loose blocky rock section with care, and anchor at the foot of the chimney that cuts its way up the second rock step.

This rock step bars the way to the final stretches to the summit, and goes at about grade IV. Naturally, grade IV in boots and crampons with a full pack containing camping gear requires slightly more focus than it would at the local crag, and the chimney does overhang at one point, just to add a bit more enjoyment and a sense of position.

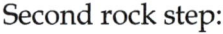
Second rock step:

From the anchor at the top of the chimney, you're back on snow, and a short but slightly tricky traverse ensues to get back onto easier ground; tricky largely because it's steep and the snow will almost certainly be soft in the sun by this stage. Continue up to the junction where the Tengu ridge (天狗尾根) joins the East ridge, and then carry on up to a small flat spot at the top of the North face. From here a final 50m ascent brings you to the North summit of Kashimayari.

Looking across to Mt Goryu from the summit:

The views from here are quite simply outstanding.

Getting down:
From the North summit, walk carefully down the slope to the col between the North and South summits. From here you have two choices:

1. Continue over the South summit, down to the site of the hut below the North summit (2631m) of Mt Jiigatake (爺ヶ岳). Then ascend a little more in the direction of Jiigatake before branching off to the west onto the Akaiwa-one (赤岩尾根) descent ridge. This ridge is a marked trail of three hours map-time in summer, and will take you all the way down to the rindou about an hour away from Ōtanbara.

2. Climb from the col between the North and South summits directly down the steep snow slopes to the east (front-pointing necessary in the upper section), and descend as quickly as you can all the way down this snow valley to the rindou at the foot of the Akaiwa-one descent ridge. Be very aware of avalanche risk if you choose to do this, and make sure that the sun has already dipped to the west behind the summit ridgeline.

Summary:
What can I say? This ridge speaks for itself, and would be a true classic anywhere in the world; the perfect route to the summit of this perfect mountain!

JAPAN EXTRAS - 8

Emergency

If things do come undone while you are out on a mountain in Japan there are a few things worth remembering. As with any other country, it is always a good idea to leave an outline of your plan with a friend, including an estimated time of return, so that they can mobilise help if you are not back in time.

As of the time of writing in 2015, the best mobile phone network in terms of signal coverage in mountainous areas in Japan is Docomo, so if you're visiting Japan for climbing and are considering renting a phone and SIM card, that's probably your best choice of network. We'd all like to see Softbank raise their game in this regard, but until that happens, I simply can't recommend them.

You should come equipped with an insurance policy to cover you for both rescue from the mountain and hospitalisation and medical treatment. Helicopter rescue is not free in certain prefectures, and does not come cheap! If you're based in Japan already, the Japan Rescue Organisation (JRO) is a co-operative group that offers a very reasonable annual policy to cover transportation from the mountain to the hospital, and is very popular amongst climbers and hikers here.

Here are a few important telephone numbers to be aware of, covering the main areas for the routes in this book:

National police number - 110
National fire / ambulance number - 119
Matsumoto police station - 026-325-0110
Nagano police station - 026-233-0110
Fujiyoshida police station - 055-221-0110
Chino police station - 0266-82-0110
Toyama police station - 076-441-2211
Minakami police station - 0278-72-2049
Ōme police station - 0428-22-0110

9. The Henkei chimney of Mt Tanigawa
谷川岳変形チムニー

Route Name: Henkei chimney (変形チムニー)

Mountain: Tanigawadake (谷川岳 1974m)

Map sheet: 16 [Yama-to-kougen-chizu (山と高原地図) series]

Length: 12 pitches

Time: 4-6 hours to the top of the last pitch

Grade: V+ (IV+ A1) crux pitch / Overall grade 4 alpine route

Getting there:
From Tokyo take the Takasaki Line for about 1.5 hours to Takasaki (高崎). Change for the Jōetsu Line for about 45 minutes to Minakami (水上), and then take a local for two stops to Doai (土合). From the underground platform at Doai station, climb a 489-step staircase from hell to reach ground level. Exit the station and join the main road, turning right and walking under a railway bridge. Follow this road for about 20 minutes up to the Visitors Centre.

Description:
Walk up the road from the Visitors Centre for about half an hour until you get to the entrance to Ichinokura-sawa (一ノ倉沢). Head up the sawa until you reach the foot of Tail ridge, and ascend this all the way to the top, at the foot of the Tsuitate (衝立岩) rock face.

From here make an exposed rising traverse to your left across the steep slabs in the direction of the Nan-ryō terrace. About two thirds of the way across you will come to the belay anchor at the bottom of the first pitch of the route.

This route is essentially a separate line for the first five pitches, after which a thinly protected but straight-forward traverse pitch brings you to the upper half of the neighbouring Chuō Kante (中央カンテ) route.

From there the two routes join, sharing the same crux pitch high up on the face. The difference though, which is what gives this route its slightly higher overall grade, is that where the first five pitches of Chuō Kante contain nothing harder than grade IV, this route passes through the magnificent Henkei chimney.

This dark and wet overhanging off-width chimney at the top of the fifth pitch goes free at V+ or aided at IV A1, and is quite simply a superb piece of climbing.

Climber in the Henkei chimney:

Approximate pitch descriptions for the route are as follows:

Pitch 1: Climb up the face on well-featured rock, taking care not to dislodge any loose stones on people below. (35m III+)

Pitch 2: Ascend up to a sort of rock flake, which turns out to be loose in its entirety, and climb it without pulling it off the mountain. Continue up for a few more metres to the belay. (30m IV)

Pitch 3: Climb the crack rising leftwards. (25m IV+)

Pitch 4: Climb easy ground up and to the right to an anchor below the chimney. (20m III)

Pitch 5: Climb up to the base of the chimney. Ascend the chimney using a variety of styles and holds, and be sure to behold the magnificent position and exposure on the final moves at the top. Belay at the anchor just out of the chimney. (20m V+ / IV A1)

Pitch 6: A straight-forward but exposed traverse to the right, to join the Chuō Kante route. Take care with loose rock. (30m III+)

Pitch 7: Up and to the right. (40m IV)

Pitch 8: Again, up and to the right. (40m III-)

Pitch 9: Climb up to the lip of the overhang, and surmount this with a strong move up on positive holds. Continue up to another leftward-rising chimney crack. Climb this chimney crack, with some layback moves, until you reach the belay at the top. (30m V+ / IV+ A1)

Pitch 10: Up and to the left. (30m IV)

Pitch 11: More up and to the left. (40m III)

Pitch 12: Ascend a few metres and traverse left, then climb up a steeper but well-featured section to gain the shoulder. The anchor at the top of the route is here, with the Eboshi (烏帽子岩) rock feature directly up on your right. (40m IV)

Descent:
From the anchor on top of the route, make a free-hanging abseil on two 50m ropes down the overhanging corner on the other side. When you touch the ground, stay connected to the ropes and continue across the slab, paying attention to loose stones, and several metres down the overgrown grassy slope on the other side of the gully to reach a dodgy piton anchor.

From this anchor you have the option of un-roping and making a sketchy traverse up and left, then down through the undergrowth to the top of the Nan-ryō (南稜) route, and many Japanese parties probably do this. Frankly speaking though, I would strongly recommend belaying this traverse. Having climbed a 12-pitch V+ rock route to get there, it would be ridiculous to slip and fall from here, and I think it would be all too easy for this to happen. It's your call, but whatever you choose, be really careful… This is a dangerous spot.

Once you get to the top of the Nan-ryō, you can traverse across to the top of the line of rappels which is the standard rappel descent. It will take you about five rappels on double ropes to reach the terrace at the start of the Nan-ryō. From here you can either unrope and downclimb or do one more rappel to easier ground. Now you just need to traverse back across to the top of Tail ridge and descend back out of Ichinokura-sawa to the road.

Summary:
A long and steep route up the striking face between the Nan-ryō (South ridge) and Chuo-ryō (Central arête) routes, with huge exposure and amazing climbing. The two crux pitches are both absolutely priceless. Bring double ropes, a full rack of slings and quickdraws, and a few small/medium cams. As always with routes in Ichinokura-sawa, be alert at all times and pay close attention to not dislodging any of the many loose rocks onto people below.

JAPAN EXTRAS - 9

The mountain hut system

Much like the European Alps, the mountains of Japan are home to an extensive network of mountain huts. They range in size and quality from small wooden unmanned emergency huts all the way to enormous sprawling constructions with television, heated baths and in some cases even free Wi-Fi. A good hut stay can really make the difference, so here are a few things you'll need to know.

The superb hut below the summit of Mt Okuhotaka:

Manned huts in Japan are privately owned and run, and generally like guests to phone and book a place in advance. If you turn up without a reservation, however, you're unlikely to be turned away, although you should aim to arrive by early evening if possible.

Typically a night in a good hut costs around ¥8000 per night including dinner. The evening meal is usually served in a dining room area around 5:30-6:30pm, and is invariably Japanese style and very good.

Most huts provide a futon and a duvet on a bunk bed or a tatami floor, usually in communal rooms. If you are staying on a bank holiday weekend, expect a lot of company! In winter the huts are often heated by kerosene stoves or jet burners. Many huts close for the winter though, so be sure to phone and check in advance. For those with their own tent, camping is usually possible in the vicinity of the hut for around ¥1000 per night.

Basic supplies can usually be purchased in huts, including alcohol and some basic foods and cup noodles. Japanese hikers tend to rise very early, and most huts will switch the lights out by about 9pm at the latest. You will normally be expected to leave, or at least vacate the bedroom, by sunrise.

The following is a selection of the huts nearest to some of the routes in this book:

Mountain	Hut	Telephone number
Yarigatake (槍ヶ岳)	Yarigatake sansou	090-2641-1911
Kitadake (北岳)	Shiraneoike-koya	90-3201-7683
Tsurugidake (剣岳)	Tsurugisawa-koya	076-482-1319
Okuhotakadake (奥穂高岳)	Okuhotakadake sansou	090-7869-0045
Maehotakadake (前穂高岳)	Karasawa hyutte	090-9002-2534
Kaikomagatake (甲斐駒ケ岳)	Shichijōdaiichi-goya	0551-42-1351

10. The Left ridge of the Chinne on Mt Tsurugi
剣岳チンネ左稜線

Route Name: Chinne left ridge (チンネ左稜線)

Mountain: Tsurugidake (剣岳 2999m)

Map sheet: 36 [Yama-to-kougen-chizu (山と高原地図) series]

Length: 13 pitches

Time: approx. five hours to the top of the last pitch

Grade: V (crux pitch) / Overall grade 4- alpine route

Mt Tsurugi (剣岳) has a fearsome reputation as one of Japan's premier mountains for alpine and rock climbers, and the route described here is one of its finest.

Situated high up near the head of the Yatsumine ridge, the Chinne (or Zinne, チンネ) is an enormous blade of rock, home to multiple hard rock climbs. The name comes from the German for "tooth", and this gives a clue to its architecture.

The classic Left Ridge (左稜線) takes the sharp edge of this blade for 13 pitches, rising steeply over knife-edges and pinnacles like the teeth on a circular saw. It is quite simply stunning. The approach is long and involved, and when you reach the top, you're still a long way from home.

Getting there:
Access to Tsurugidake requires getting up to Murodō (室堂) on the large plateau below the summit of Tateyama (立山) in the North Alps. If travelling from Tokyo on public transport there are a couple of ways you can do this, none of them easy, but the quickest and cheapest way is as follows.

Take a Chūō Line limited express Super Azusa from Shinjuku station to Matsumoto (松本), then change onto the Ōito Line (大糸線) for a local train to Shinano-Ōmachi (信濃大町).

From there you'll need to take a bus to Ōgisawa (扇沢, 45mins, ¥1330). At Ōgisawa, queue up at the ticket office and buy a return ticket for the Tateyama Kurobe Alpine Route (立山黒部アルペンルート).

This convoluted but impressive series of stages will take you through a trolley bus up to the famous Kurobe Dam (黒部ダム), followed by a funicular railway, a ropeway and then a final trolley bus through Mt Tateyama to Murodō.

From Murodō head out of the top station and find the most direct way through the maze of trails through Jigokudani, down to the campsite at the valley floor, and then up the trail on the other side to the Tsurugigozen (剣御前) hut up on the col. From there a short walk will bring you down to the Tsurugi-sawa camp ground (剣沢キャンプ場).

The approach:
There are a few ways you could tackle the approach to this route. Many climbers continue down Tsurugi-sawa past the campsite, down round the foot of the Genjiro ridge (源次郎尾根), and then up into the Choujiro-dani (長次郎谷), the large valley dropping down from the summit ridge flanked by the Genjiro and Yatsumine ridges on the left and right respectively.

Midway up the valley is a flat area large enough for quite a few tents, known as Kuma-no-iwa. The advantage of a night spent here is that the approach to the summit ridge and the start of the route the next morning is relatively short.

The grandiose Yatsumine ridge flanking Choujiro-dani:

Another option is to follow the normal hiking trail up towards the summit of Mt Tsurugi, and bivouac as high up as you can get on your travel day. The summit of Mt Mae-Tsurugi (前剣) has ample space for two or three people to bivvy comfortably, and you could leave your bivvy gear there to pick up on your return.

From the bivvy site you need to get over the summit of Tsurugi the next morning, and then pick your way carefully along the ridgeline beyond the summit over to a small col at the top of the Choujiro-dani below the final pinnacle on the Yatsumine ridge.

From there head left and scramble down a steep scree slope for about 1-200m and then traverse across to the San-no-mado (三の窓) col on your right. There is also space for a tent on this col, and the views are absolutely magnificent.

From the San-no-mado col you need to head to your right and traverse across under the imposing rock face of the Chinne until you come to a ledge at the bottom of the first pitch.

Route description:
The topo cites 13 pitches from bottom to top. Some of them are fairly short and could be linked together, but be careful with communication, as the route occasionally disappears round the corner to the other side of the ridge.

On the whole the climbing is moderate and steady, never exceeding an average of grade III/IV, except for the crux pitch about two thirds up the route.

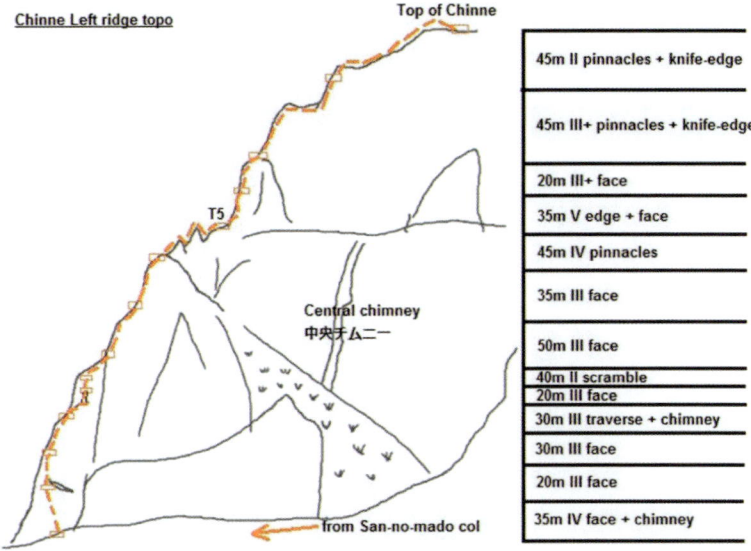

Approximate pitch descriptions for the route are as follows:

Pitch 1: Climb the face to the start of the chimney crack. Make an interesting move to enter a short chimney crack, then continue to belay on the ledge above. (35m IV)

Pitch 2: Face climbing. (20m III)

Pitch 3: Face climbing. (30m III)

Pitch 4: A short traverse to climber's right, followed by a chimney crack. (30m III)

Pitch 5: Face climbing. (20m III)

Pitch 6: Easy scramble across a fairly gentle tree-covered ridge. (40m II)

Pitch 7: Face climbing with a lot of loose rock around. (50m II/III)

Pitch 8: Face climbing. (35m III)

Pitch 9: Short descent into the gap, then a steep crack to gain the top of a pinnacle, then over another easier pinnacle to belay on the terrace at the foot of the crux pitch. (45m IV)

Traversing the teeth of the Chinne:

Pitch 10: Climb the right edge, then overcome two small overhangs (can be aided on in-situ pitons if needed) and continue up steep and interesting face climbing. (35m V)

Pitch 11: Face climbing. (20m III+)

Pitch 12: Pinnacles and knife-edge. (45m III+)

Pitch 13: Pinnacles and knife-edge. (45m II)

Descent:
From the top of the Chinne, a short down-climb brings you to a notch in the ridgeline, above the summit of the equally impressive Cleopatra Needle.

Scramble down the far side, with rappel anchors if needed, to regain the scree gully. Ascend the scree to the top, and then reverse your approach from the morning.

Summary:
One of Japan's king lines, and situated near the summit of its finest mountain too. Bring a full rack of quickdraws and a selection of nuts and cams. Don't forget your game face because it's a long trip, any way you slice it.

Appendix 1: Glossary of Japanese mountain words

Topography:

mountain	yama	山
peak	take/dake	岳
summit	chōjō	頂上
ridge	one	尾根
arête	ryō	稜
valley	tani/dani	谷
gully	runze	ルンゼ
waterfall	taki	滝
rock	iwa	岩
alps	arupusu	アルプス
forest	mori	森
pass	tōge	峠
river	kawa/gawa	川
stream	sawa	沢

Infrastructure:

mountain hut	yama-goya	山小屋
lodge	sansō	山荘
cable car	ropuei	ロープウェイ
trailhead	tozan-guchi	登山口
station (e.g. Fuji 5th station)	gōme	号目
camp ground	kyampu-jō	キャンプ場
mountain/forest road	rindou	リンドウ

Weather:

rain	ame	雨
snow	yuki	雪
ice	kōri	氷
wind	kaze	風
sunny	hare	晴れ
cloudy	kumori	曇り
weather	tenki	天気

Navigation:

north	*kita*	北
south	*minami*	南
east	*higashi*	東
west	*nishi*	西
straight on	*massugu*	まっすぐ
left	*hidari*	左
right	*migi*	右
up	*ue*	上
down	*shita*	下
in front	*mae*	前
behind	*ushiro*	後ろ

General:

prefecture	*ken*	件
shrine	*jinja*	神社
avalanche	*nadare*	なだれ
crampons	*aizen*	アイゼン
ice axe	*pikkeru*	ピッケル
map	*chizu*	地図
rope	*rōpu*	ロープ

Appendix 2: Route log

Use this section to record the details of your ascents for later in life when memory begins to fade.

	Mountain	Route name	Date	Partner
1	Yarigatake (槍ヶ岳)	Kitakama ridge (北鎌尾根)		
	Notes			
2	Tanigawadake (谷川岳)	South ridge (南稜)		
	Notes			
3	Maehotakadake (前穂高岳)	North ridge (北尾根)		
	Notes			
4	Tanigawadake (谷川岳)	Central arête (中央稜)		
	Notes			
5	Shiroumadake (白馬岳)	Main ridge (主稜)		
	Notes			

	Mountain	Route name	Date	Partner
6	Kitadake (北岳)	Buttress No4 ridge (第四尾根 バットレス)		
	Notes			
7	Kaikomagatake (甲斐駒ケ岳)	O-ren-dani right fork (黄蓮谷右俣)		
	Notes			
8	Kashimayarigatake (鹿島槍ヶ岳)	East ridge (東尾根)		
	Notes			
9	Tanigawadake (谷川岳)	Henkei chimney (変形チムニー)		
	Notes			
10	Tsurugidake (剣岳)	Chinne Left ridge (チンネ左稜線)		
	Notes			

Appendix 3: Selected additional climbs

Use this section as a springboard for ideas for more climbing routes and further research. Routes are grouped by area, or mountain range.

The NORTH ALPS

- Mt Tsurugi (剣岳 2999m)

A: Genjiro ridge (源次郎尾根)

In summer the Genjiro is a popular rock scramble with a rappel midway. In spring conditions it is a classic snow ridge with knife-edge sections. For bonus points it finishes right on the summit, from where the normal hiking trail descent will bring you back into Tsurugi-sawa.

B: Yatsumine ridge (八ツ峰主稜)

One of the most recognisable pieces of Tsurugi's architecture, the Yatsumine is both long and committing. Although in summer it can feasibly be climbed without a rope except for the rappels, in spring the conditions will dictate everything. It can range from comfortable to extremely committing and adventurous. This is a very big line on a serious mountain.

- Mt Kasumizawa (霞沢岳 2646m)

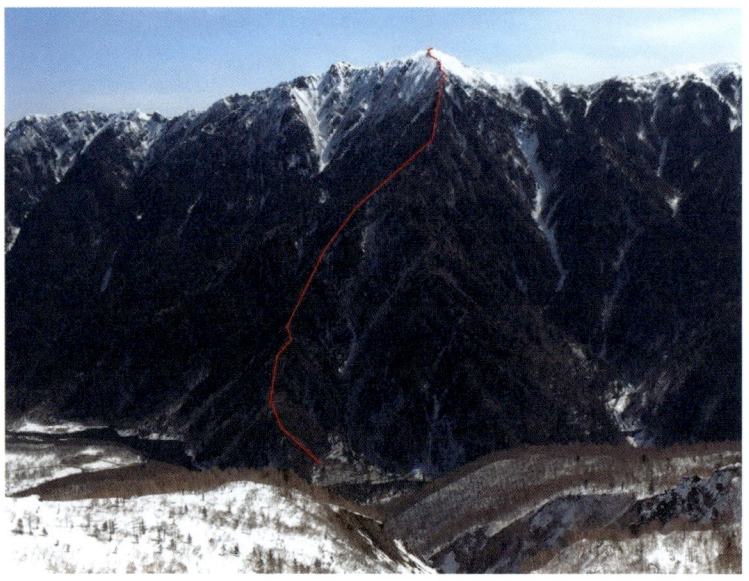

West ridge (西尾根)

This beautiful mountain sits opposite Mt Yake at the head of the valley above Kamikōchi resort. Its W ridge is essentially a steep hike up forested terrain until you break tree line. From there on a beautiful narrow snow ridge snakes upwards with a grade II rock step barring the final summit slopes.
This side of Mt Kasumizawa is only really climbable in winter, and comes highly recommended for its 360 degree summit panorama.

- Mt Jii (爺ヶ岳 2669m)

East ridge (東稜)

Accessed from Kashimayari village, the first half of this route is rather physical, involving full-body bushwhacking up steep sasa-covered ridgeline. Once you break tree line, however, the area opens up and the views are outstanding. Follow the ridge over several large pinnacles, with one 10m knife-edge traverse, until a shoulder is reached. From there the ridge swings to climber's right for the final ascent to the 2667m Central summit of Mt Jii (or Jiigatake).

Options for descent are either to reverse the ridge, or to continue over the N summit and down to the top of the Akaiwa ridge, which brings you steeply down to the river and out to Otanbara trailhead.

Overall this is a lovely snow ridge with more moderate difficulties than the neighbouring E ridge of Kashimayari.

- Mt Maehotaka (前穂高岳 3090m)

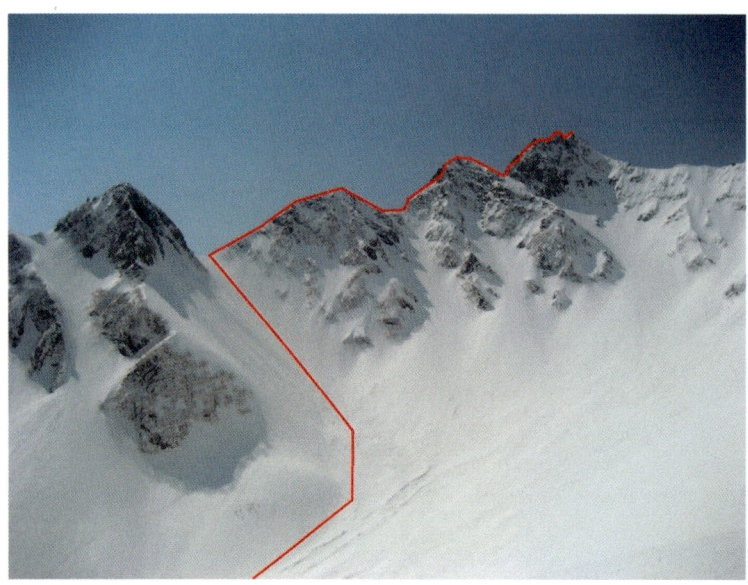

North ridge (北尾根)

Already covered in this book as a summer route, this iconic ridgeline can also be climbed as a spring mixed snow and rock route. Access is generally from Karasawa valley via the 5-6 col. Care must be taken with avalanche risk on the approach.

The chimney is the normal way through the crux section low down on P3 in snow conditions.

From the summit the normal descent is to traverse along the Tsuri ridge to the top of Okuhotaka, and then drop back down into Karasawa from there.

- Byoubu-iwa (屏風岩)

This striking rock face is visible on your left as you ascend into Karasawa valley, and is home to many multi-pitch climbs. Routes here are predominantly aid-climbing, but this might be due to the limitations of the equipment and techniques in the era they were first climbed.

Be careful with the in-situ protection though… Rusty pitons and ring bolts still abound from those old days.

From the summit, a short scramble will bring you down to the Panorama hiking trail at the end of the Maehotaka N ridge, and from there you can walk back down to the river and Kamikōchi.

Byoubu-iwa might be one of the closest things Japan has to a big wall.

The SOUTH ALPS

- Mt Kaikoma (甲斐駒ケ岳 2967m)

Todai-gawa hondani (戸台川本谷)

This route requires a very long approach up the Todai river on the West side of Mt Kaikoma, which probably explains why it receives far fewer attempts than the O-ren-dani. Parties usually bivvy at the entrance to the hondani, or about an hour up the sawa at the first icefall.

Difficulties are generally in the WI 3-4 range, but interesting route-finding through complex terrain raises the stakes.

In the eventuality of an accident, rescue on this side of the mountain would be a highly involved affair, which makes this a route not to be taken too lightly in spite of its moderate grading.

- Mt Nokogiri (鋸山 2685m)

The Sawtooth ridge traverse

Access to Mt Nokogiri from the Todai river is an event in itself, involving several hours of toil up a gigantic scree field, through rocks perched on top of rocks at the angle of repose. Once there the traverse of the Sawtooth ridge over to Mt Kaikoma is its own reward. Scrambling over exposed teeth and pinnacles, and through the famous Shika-no-mado gap, is pure joy!

Make no mistake though… This is a big day out, so bring plenty of energy. From the summit of Kaikoma you can either descend the Kuroto ridge to the East, or take the shorter trail to the Kitazawa pass.

This traverse also provides a grade 1 alpine outing in winter, and a bivvy is necessary for most teams. It is not uncommon for a winter traverse to stretch to three days due to the length of the approach.

The YATSUGATAKE massif (八ヶ岳 2899m)

- Akadake-kousen area

A: The Uradoushin gully (裏同心ルンゼ)

A classic introduction to Japanese winter sawa-climbing, the Uradoushin features five icefalls connected by progressively steeper snow slopes. The crux F5 icefall goes at WI 3 or 4, depending on conditions. A 50m rope and a rack of screws will be plenty. To descend, traverse across under the Daidoushin pinnacle to the top of the Daidoushin ridge, and hike back down to the Akadake-kousen hut.

B: Daidoushin ridge (大同心稜)

An initial hike up a forested ridgeline brings you to the large Daidoushin rock pinnacle. Skirt under the bottom of the pinnacle, and ascend the mixed terrain around the back to the top. From the summit ridgeline, either head north to Iodake and down, or south over Yokodake.

C: Daidoushin gully (大同心ルンゼ)

This route is similar to the Uradoushin gully until you reach its centerpiece, the 55m WI5 Daidoushin Ōtaki icefall. Most people rappel the Ōtaki and walk back down, but it's possible to continue up to access the top half of the Daidoushin ridge.

D: Daidoushin pinnacle South ridge (大同心南稜)

This 3-pitch route is climbed in summer or winter to the top of the pinnacle. The final pitch is given a grade of IV A1, with in-situ gear to aid up. Be careful of loose rock in summer.

E: Shodoushin crack (小同心クラック)

This is a 3-pitch route at IV- up the chimney that cleaves the front of the Shodoushin pinnacle. Clearly visible from the Akadake-kousen hut, it too can be climbed in summer or winter.

F: Sansahou gully (三叉峰ルンゼ)

Conditions on this classic stepped ice route up the centre of the face below Yokodake can be rather fickle, with some years seeing it unformed all season. But when it's in, it's a fantastic route with a great Scottish feel to it. From the top of the ice, ascend the snow slopes above to a long traverse right of the Sekison ridge, then climb mixed ground to gain the summit ridgeline.

G: Sekison ridge (石尊稜)

This moderate mixed ridge is a popular one among the Japanese guides. An initial grade III rock slab gains a snow arête that leads up to a final III mixed rock step to the summit ridgeline. In good conditions it will only take a couple of hours to climb, leaving time for something else.

H: Nakayama ridge (中山尾根)

More serious than its neighbour, the Nakayama ridge is a rocky arête with two main rock steps going at III+ (lower step) and IV+ (upper step) respectively. A dramatic finish brings you to the summit ridgeline with great views of the nearby West face of Mt Aka. This route is deservedly popular.

- Mt Amida (阿弥陀岳 2805m)

A: North ridge (北稜)

The easiest of Amida's variation ridges, the North ridge is an enjoyable climb up a snow arête to a couple of rock steps (grade III and grade II) which gain access to the upper ridge.

B: Northwest ridge (北西稜)

This is a classic mixed ridge, with seven pitches of rock and a crux of III A1. There is in-situ protection, and good belay anchors. The position and the climbing are first-rate.

From the summit, the normal hiking trail will bring you back down to the Gyojagoya hut. Pay attention to avalanche conditions here in mid-winter.

GUNMA prefecture

- Mt Tanigawa (谷川岳 1974m)

As you ascend Tail ridge to access the three classic routes described in this book, the eye is drawn across the breathtaking face of the triangular monolith on your right. Consistently vertical, and overhanging in many places, this face of the Tsuitate-iwa is home to several legendary hard rock climbs.

1: Cloud ridge first route (雲稜第一ルート)

This 9-pitch route takes the series of roofs left of centre, and is the classic hard rock climb in the area from the heyday of Tanigawa climbing in the late 1950s. If climbed free it contains four pitches between 5.11a and 5.11d, and one pitch of 5.10d. But this is not solid Yosemite granite; rather it is the loose chossy rock that is typical of Tanigawa. It's a monster!

2: Cloud ridge second route (雲稜第二ルート)

This right-hand route takes the line of the largest overhangs up the right side of the face, and is typically aid-climbed. Once again loose rock, difficult climbing and a storied history make this an intimidating route.

The East ridge (東尾根)

Climbed in both summer and winter, this ridge forms the right flank of Machiga-sawa and the left flank of Ichinokura-sawa, and provides an interesting and moderate outing with plenty of exposure and adventure.

The route begins at the Shinsen col, although access in summer and winter is from different sides of the ridge (Machiga-sawa and Ichinokura-sawa respectively).

- Mt Komochi (子持山 1296m)

Shishi-iwa (獅子岩)

Shishi-iwa, or 'Lion rock', is distinctly visible high on the shoulder of Mt Komochi from across the valley as you drive up the Kanetsu Expressway in the direction of Mt Tanigawa. It is home to a lovely 6-pitch route on very good quality friction rock, mostly slab and face climbing.

The route is of moderate difficulty, mostly 5.7 with a crux pitch of 5.8.

The approach involves an easy hike of about an hour from the car park, and descent from the top of the rock is by way of the normal hiking trail.

Get there early because this is a deservedly popular route among local climbers and Tokyo climbers alike.

NIIGATA prefecture

- Mt Makihata (巻機山 1967m)

Nukubi-zawa (ヌクビ沢)

Sitting close to the Gunma/Niigata prefectural border, approximately midway between Mt Tanigawa (谷川岳) and Mt Echigo-Komagatake (越後駒ヶ岳), it is no surprise that Mt Makihata gets buried under metres of snow every winter.

By early summer, not all of that snow has melted. With steep walls on either side shading it for much of the day, and the impressive Tengu (天狗岩) rock formation guarding its upper reaches, the Nukubi-zawa river course holds its snow almost year-round.

Whilst not strictly an alpine variation route, the Nukubi-zawa is a step-up from an ordinary hiking trail.

It may require some basic rope skills and equipment depending on conditions, which could vary wildly from month to month and year to year. It would be prudent not to try it during the rainy season, but from mid-July onwards it's game on.

The later you leave it, the less snow and the more dry rock you're going to find. But for my money early summer is where it's at, when you can enjoy a cool breeze wafting down the snow fields while all around the earth is baking.

CHICHIBU-TAMA National Park

- Mt Futago (二子山 1165m)

Central arête (中央稜)

This fine 7-pitch rock route up the striking Central arête contains a mix of easy and harder pitches. The difficulties are all focused in its lower half, including the striking triangular rock flake for which the route is famous.

The higher you progress the more the route and the face open up, providing a sense of depth to the valley falling away below.

The Central arête is a moderate route, its crux weighing in at 5.9 A0 and the remainder of its pitches around 5.7-5.8. For those looking for something more testing, however, Futagoyama is home to plentiful limestone rock-climbing, including Yuji Hirayama's famous 5.15a 'Flat Mountain'.

For my money though, if you can get this route to yourselves on a weekday or early morning the Central arête is one of the finest multi-pitch rock routes within easy striking distance of Tokyo by car.

The crux pitch of the Central arête:

Further information

The routes in this book should give you a strong flavour of the kind of alpine climbing that exists in Japan. However, it is by no means exhaustive. The Japanese archipelago is literally covered in mountains, and the sheer amount of climbing, hiking, trail running, sawanobori and ice-climbing to be had on these islands is mind-boggling.

You will find a lot more information and route descriptions on my website, Climb Japan, covering a range of activity types at all times of the year.

www.climbjapan.blogspot.com

In addition to this stay tuned for further titles in the Climb Japan series. The next book will be an in-depth guide to climbing and hiking in the popular Yatsugatake mountain range in Yamanashi prefecture.

If you have enjoyed this book and found it useful, please consider leaving a review and rating in your favourite retail store.

Many thanks!

Acknowledgements

There are many things that go into the creation of a book like this, and the actual writing itself is just the final stage in a long process. Along the way the list of people who have supported me directly or indirectly has grown inordinately, so I will do my best to remember you all here, and I apologise to anyone who I have left out.

To the friends who have partnered me on the routes in this book and on the many other memorable climbs I've done in Japan, and graciously supplied their photos of these climbs, I salute you all; Rod Szasz, Alan Tomlinson, Julian Ross, Chris White, Michael O'Shaugnessy, Ed Hannam, Tracy Lenard, Tomohiro Kanezaki, Sano-san, Chikatsu Nakajima, Takahiro Shinozaki, Jacques Lalancette, Paul Manson, David Niehoff, Gint Atkinson, Chris Harris.

Finally the most important contribution to be acknowledged is the patience and encouragement of my wife, Mika. Without your support over the years, none of this would have been possible.

Tony Grant (Jan 2016)

Notes

Notes

Notes

Notes

Notes

Notes

Printed in Great Britain
by Amazon